PUB STROLLS IN
MIDDLESEX & WEST LONDON

David Hall and Rosemary Hall

COUNTRYSIDE BOOKS
NEWBURY BERKSHIRE

COUNTRYSIDE BOOKS
3 Catherine Road
Newbury, Berkshire

To view our complete range of books,
please visit us at
www.countrysidebooks.co.uk

ISBN 1 85306 728 8

*For Rosemary's mother, Alice Hall, who always
encouraged Rosemary in her ventures.*

Photographs by the authors

Produced through MRM Associates Ltd., Reading
Printed in Italy

Contents

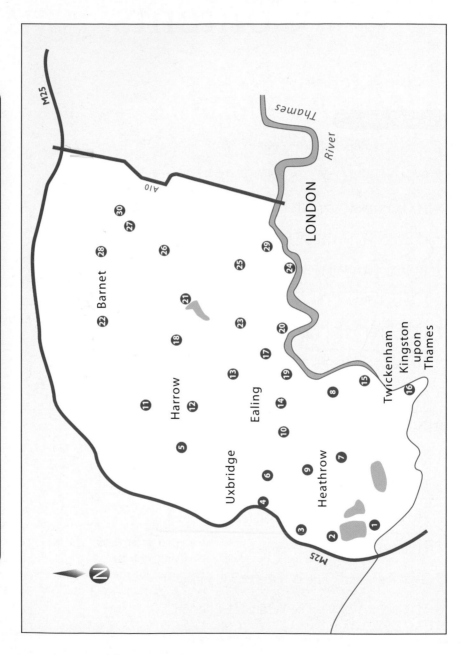

AREA MAP SHOWING LOCATION OF THE WALKS

PUBLISHER'S NOTE

We hope that you obtain considerable enjoyment from this book; great care has been taken in its preparation. Although at the time of publication all routes followed public rights of way or permitted paths, diversion orders can be made and permissions withdrawn.

We cannot, of course, be held responsible for such diversion orders and any inaccuracies in the text which result from these or any other changes to the routes nor any damage which might result from walkers trespassing on private property. We are anxious, though, that all details covering the walks are kept up to date and would therefore welcome information from readers which would be relevant to future editions.

The simple sketch maps that accompany the walks in this book are based on notes made by the authors whilst checking out the routes on the ground. However, for the benefit of a proper map, we do recommend that you purchase the relevant Ordnance Survey sheet covering your walk. The Ordnance Survey maps are widely available, especially through booksellers and local newsagents.

Middlesex – the big banana round the edge of London. That's the shape of the old county described pretty accurately by a friend. So here, scattered about the banana, from Staines to Barnet, are thirty pubs and thirty very pleasant strolls in some of the astonishing amount of green space to be found in and around our capital city.

The walks are quite short, averaging three miles, and we've concentrated on making them as enjoyable as possible. There are strolls down by the Thames; on Horsenden Hill; around Harrow on the Hill; in urban nature reserves; through an old cemetery; past Wren's spectacular Royal Hospital, home of the Chelsea Pensioners; and in parts of London so rural you'd think you were in the country.

We do not drive, so we used public transport and tell you how to do the same. Our advice is to leave the car at home, and enjoy the pubs we've found as starting points for the strolls. Most of the pubs are new to us, many are quite special in one way or another, and all offer a warm welcome. You'll find food in all of them, from honest to goodness 'pub grub' to upmarket 'gastropub' dishes. There's a wonderful choice of pub names, too – the traditional, such as The Green Man, three with bells in the name, and some we just had to include: The Catcher in the Rye and Paradise by Way of Kensal Green, for example. Many of them are worth visiting for their own sake.

The names of local churches varied less. 'St Mary's' is the typical name for a Middlesex parish church, being twice as frequent as the next most popular saint. We haven't noticed this trend elsewhere. Does anyone know why this is?

If you do take the car and want to leave it in the pub car park, please ask first, even where we say it's okay to do so. Unless stated otherwise, the pubs are open all day, which means 11 am to 11 pm from Monday to Saturday and 12 noon to 10.30 pm on Sunday. Do check, though, if you are relying on a drink or a meal, particularly on a weekday afternoon in January.

We must thank our long-suffering families and friends (and editors). Rosemary thanks particularly: the wardens of East Bedfont Country Park, Cranford Park and, especially, Hounslow Heath, for assistance when lost; Nick Chasey and Tony Peacock, for directions from Staines Moor back to Staines before dark, and for recommending The Bells; Beth Scott, for the same pub; Bob Dunne and David Sharp, at the Welsh Harp, for information and a map; Valerie Robertson, head of St Eugene's, for allowing her to escape the classroom and walk on sunny days; and Kathleen and Emma O'Conner for the pub recommendations. Especial thanks from David to: Sarah Helpin, paradisal publican; the staff at Harmondsworth Moor Visitor Centre; Karalyn Foord, the summer warden at Gunnersbury Triangle; Catherine and Stephen for selflessly assisting with pub research; and his wife, Janet, for assisting with research, blackberries, last-minute pruning and magical transformations.

Finally, enjoy the walks and pubs – we did.

David Hall
Rosemary Hall

Staines
The Bells

MAP: OS EXPLORER 160 (GR 032716)   **WALK 1**   **DISTANCE:** 2½ MILES

DIRECTIONS TO START: THE PUB IS AT 124 CHURCH STREET, STAINES. FROM LONDON, HEAD INTO STAINES ON LONDON ROAD (A308), FOLLOW THE ONE-WAY SYSTEM ROUND SOUTH STREET, PAST THE BUS STATION, AND TURN RIGHT BEFORE THE BRIDGE. **STATION:** STAINES. **PARKING:** THERE IS A CAR PARK AT THE PUB. ALTERNATIVELY USE THE LARGE PAY & DISPLAY CAR PARK AT THE TWO RIVERS SHOPPING CENTRE.

Lakes, rivers, reservoirs and Staines Moor endow this area – though close to Heathrow Airport and the M25 – with a great variety of birds, wildflowers and insects. This stroll is full of interest. After taking a winding path around several lakes you proceed to Staines Moor where you walk beside the meandering River Colne. The moor is ancient common land and was designated one of the UK's first Sites of Special Scientific Interest. You return to the pub along a leafy path by the Wraysbury River.

The Bells

This cosy and welcoming Young's pub has a comfortably furnished, carpeted bar with a pleasing mellow décor at the front and two dining areas at the back. One dining room is in a covered flagstone courtyard, which leads into a well-kept garden. Young's Bitter and Special are on handpump and there is a range of bottled lagers and a good selection of wines. The hand-written menu changes daily but offerings may include starters of chilled melon, feta cheese salad or deep fried whitebait; mains of fillet steak, roast leg of lamb, turkey and ham pie or cheese and onion flan; and puddings of fresh fruit salad, chocolate fudge cake or cherry cheese cake. At least two vegetarian main courses feature every day. The pub keeps standard pub hours and food is served from 12 noon to 2.30 pm and 6.30 pm to 9 pm on Monday to Saturday. Sunday lunch is served from 12 noon to 3 pm but there is no food on Sunday evenings. Children are welcome if they are eating. Telephone: 01784 454240.

The Walk

① Leave the pub and turn left along Church Street. Cross the end of Island Close and pass the bridge to Church Island on the left. Turn left though a black metal gate and continue ahead along the gravel riverside path. At the end of this path turn right into Lammas Recreation Ground. Continue ahead passing tennis courts on the right and playing fields on the left.

② Leave the recreation ground, cross Wraysbury Road and turn left through a

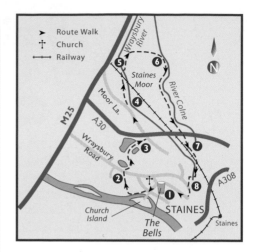

metal barrier into Church Lammas. Take the main path, which veers right, then left, then winds among three ponds and eventually veers right to go to the right of metal railings.

③ Turn left over a stile and just before the tunnel ascend the steps to a tarmac T-junction. Turn right and continue ahead. Go through a wooden barrier. At Moor Lane turn left, go under the bridge and continue along the left-hand pavement.

④ Just beyond the Swan pub on the left, and 10 yards beyond a drinking fountain on the right, veer right onto a poorly defined path signposted 'Footpath to Stanwell Moor 2'. Continue through a wooden kissing gate, over a railway line (taking care) and through another kissing gate. Veer slightly left and go ahead on the path passing an electricity pylon on the left. Walk along a wooden ramp and turn right over a bridge to cross the Wraysbury River. Keep straight on at the fork just ahead (veering right goes under a tunnel), with the M25 to the left and ahead.

On Staines Moor

⑤ Before the path veers left through a wide gap in wooden railings, look for a stile across the grass on the right – this is not obvious. Turn right, cross the stile and go ahead up a steep path. At the T-junction, turn left along the gravel track, a former railway line. Ignore a poorly defined path to the left and, just three yards further on, take a poorly defined path to the right. Go over a wooden footbridge, a ditch and a stile onto Staines Moor. Continue across the moor, away from the M25.

⑥ Turn right at the River Colne and continue along its right bank, staying close to the river. Pass a bridge over the river (don't cross) and later, on the right, an electricity pylon. Leave the moor through a wooden kissing gate. Go under the A30 and through another kissing gate. Take the narrow path across grass, and then between metal railings to cross a brick footbridge over the River Ash.

⑦ At the fork veer right across a stile. Continue ahead across a second stile and, taking care, cross the railway line. Go over a third stile and turn left along the path between the railway line on the left and the Wraysbury River on the right. Continue on the tarmac path to veer left and then right over a wooden footbridge crossing the river. Continue ahead to the right of the car park.

⑧ Turn left onto Wraysbury Road and then right at the traffic lights to cross it. Turn left to continue in the same direction, following the road as it curves right. Veer right onto Church Street and continue to the pub on the left.

PLACES OF INTEREST NEARBY

The **Spelthorne Museum** is on Market Square in Staines. Opening times are Wednesday and Friday 2 pm to 4 pm and Saturday 1.30 pm to 4.30 pm. Telephone: 01784 461804. **Thorpe Park**, 4 miles south of Staines on Staines Road at Chertsey, is a large theme park developed around several gravel-pit lakes and renowned for its 'white-knuckle' rides. There is a frequent bus service from Staines. Telephone: 01932 562633.

Stanwell Moor
The Anchor

DIRECTIONS TO START: THE PUB IS ON HORTON ROAD, STANWELL MOOR. TAKE HORTON ROAD OFF THE M25 AT JUNCTION 14 (DO NOT TAKE THE A3113) AND FOLLOW THIS EAST INTO STANWELL MOOR STRAIGHT TO THE PUB. **STATION:** STAINES. BUS: 555 FROM ASHFORD TO JUNCTION OF STANWELL MOOR ROAD AND HORTON ROAD. **PARKING:** IN THE PUB CAR PARK, OR ROADSIDE PARKING.

This stroll from the friendly Anchor pub in Stanwell Moor takes you beside a reservoir and two rivers and over a Site of Special Scientific Interest where a number of rare plants may be seen. You start off on a former railway track by the Wraysbury River, a useful green corridor. The route continues over Staines Moor (see also Walk 1) where many species of birds have been recorded in recent years. You return to the pub alongside the River Colne, passing a favourite spot for swans, and then on the perimeter path of the King George VI Reservoir.

The Anchor

This is a Greene King house in a village somewhat cut off by Heathrow Airport, reservoirs and the M25, but treasured by regulars. It is a welcoming place with a garden at the back and a large and comfortable bar where food is available. The public bar to the left of the entrance has wooden floorboards and there is a raised dining area to the right. The menu includes burgers, ham, egg and chips, cod and chicken Kiev as well as jacket potatoes with a variety of fillings, sandwiches and ploughman's lunches. At least two daily specials are on offer as well as a range of desserts. Children are welcome for meals.

The pub is open from 12 noon (note the late start) to 11 pm, 10.30 pm on Sundays. Food is served from 12 noon to 2 pm on Monday to Friday and Sunday. Beers on handpump are Ruddles County and Greene King IPA. Telephone: 01753 682707.

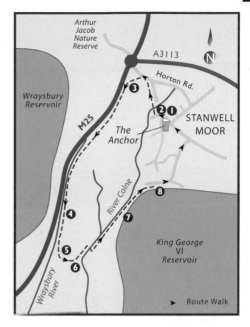

The Walk

① Leave the pub and turn left to walk along Hithermoor Lane. When Hithermoor Lane veers left continue ahead along Leylands Lane.

② When the road veers left, go straight ahead across a wooden footbridge and turn right and go over another bridge. Both bridges cross weirs. Continue ahead along a path to the left of the River Colne. Continue ahead on the road when the path ends, ignoring a turn left and passing a caravan park on the right.

③ Just before the T-junction turn left on a narrow tarmac path. Continue ahead when the tarmac becomes a dirt track and then a wide metalled track. This path runs parallel and to the left of the M25 and then the Wraysbury River and is a former railway line. It was opened in 1885 to connect Staines to the GWR at West Drayton. The line was closed in 1965. Eventually pass metal railings around Moor Lane reservoir shaft on the right.

④ Shortly after passing a brick hut on the right veer left to go through a gap to the right of a wide wooden gate and continue ahead on an earth path.

⑤ Shortly, at a crosspaths, turn left and go between wooden posts onto Staines Moor. Continue ahead, keeping on this main path. Eventually you will see the River

The River Colne

Colne ahead and to the right. Continue to the river – you should reach it at quite a sharp bend where there are often swans to be seen.

⑥ Turn left and walk by the river, then turn right across the bridge. Turn left at the other side to follow a yellow arrow on a post along the right side of the river. Continue ahead, cross a wooden footbridge over Bonehead Ditch and go through a narrow gate and metal barrier. Continue ahead on this path.

⑦ At the two-armed Colne Valley Way sign turn left to follow the concrete path around the embankment of the King George VI Reservoir. Continue ahead over a concrete footbridge to the end of the path.

⑧ Turn right onto Hithermoor Road. The houses on the right are set back from the road behind one of the ubiquitous brooks here. Continue ahead and at the T-junction turn left onto Horton Road and back to the pub.

PLACES OF INTEREST NEARBY

Windsor is just 6 miles to the west. Apart from the obvious attraction of the castle and historic town centre, there are several small museums. Telephone the Windsor Tourist Information Centre on 01753 743900 for further details. Within walking distance of Stanwell Moor, off the north side of Horton Road, Poyle, is the **Arthur Jacob Nature Reserve**, a wetland reserve with four lagoons, dipping platforms, a bird hide and a variety of trees, shrubs and wildflowers.

Harmondsworth Moor
The Five Bells

MAP: OS EXPLORER 160 (GR 057778)

WALK 3

DISTANCE: 2 MILES

DIRECTIONS TO START: THE PUB IS RIGHT IN THE VILLAGE AT THE END OF THE HIGH STREET WHICH IS OFF THE A3044. **STATIONS:** WEST DRAYTON (SUBURBAN RAIL), WALK OR BUS U3 TO HARMONDSWORTH; HATTON CROSS (PICCADILLY) BUS H30 TO WATERSIDE (BA HQ). **PARKING:** THERE IS LITTLE PARKING IN THE VILLAGE; CAR PARKING IS PROVIDED ON THE MOOR OFF ACCOMMODATION LANE, REACHED VIA TARMAC WAY FROM THE A4.

Harmondsworth Moor is a large countryside park cut off from the outside world by motorways, the A4 and Heathrow Airport. It is full of wildlife, ponds, lakes, meadows with wildflowers, and woods of native trees. You may see kestrels and foxes. Situated next to the peaceful village of Harmondsworth, it makes a wonderful place to walk. Yet you won't find it on most maps. It has been constructed over the last few years from reclaimed land by British Airways, whose headquarters, Waterside, is here by Swan Lake, which actually does have swans. Just a few years ago that part of the site was a scrubby field, but Swan Lake is all about magical transformations.

The Five Bells

The pub has a very attractive position at the end of the village green next to the church. There is a lounge bar and a games bar, with a few tables tucked away into nooks and crannies. The large garden is filled with tables and is very pleasant in summer. An extensive menu of starters and main courses includes traditional pub favourites, such as omelettes, burgers and fish and chicken dishes, and one or two more unusual choices such as vegetarian Thai curry, and there is a Sunday roast. If you're not after a full meal the filled baguettes and sandwiches are very generous. The pub is popular with airport staff, and can be busy at lunchtime. Food is available until about 3 pm, and some evenings, but check for availability. The beers kept are Adnams Bitter and Broadside, Fuller's London Pride and Wychwood Shires. Telephone: 020 8759 4713.

The Walk

① Leave the pub, turn right down Moor Lane, cross the bridge over the Duke of Northumberland's River and turn left through the kissing gate into Harmondsworth Moor. Walk towards Swan Lake, and Waterside, BA's headquarters. Turn right at the lake, and follow the lakeside round to the visitor centre (open from 4 pm to 6 pm on weekdays and from 2 pm to 4 pm at weekends, telephone: 020 8738 9596). The Park Rangers keep a record of bird sightings at the visitor centre. Jays, chaffinches and redwings are frequently seen, and kingfishers and warblers less often. Leave this part of the park via the

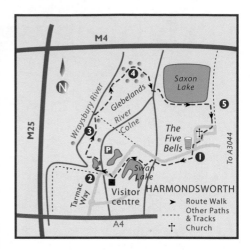

visitor centre car park and gates, turn left onto Accommodation Lane and cross the River Colne.

② Immediately after the river, cross the road and go through the kissing gate onto the continuation of Accommodation Lane as a grassy track. After less than 30 yards, turn right through the first kissing gate and follow the path across the footbridge into Middle Meadow. Turn right at the small lake, and follow the path round it – the River Colne is on your right. At a bench, turn left to follow the path over the lake. Keep left over a wooden bridge, turn right at a wooden fence and follow a broader path uphill. Head north along the ridge, through meadows with wildflowers, passing woods.

③ Pass a memorial to the seven crew of a Canadian bomber that crashed here in 1943. Fork left and walk down between two fenced wooded areas. Turn right at a fence in front of the Wraysbury River. Go through a kissing gate, cross the track, and go through the kissing gate opposite into

Middle Meadow

Glebelands. Follow the path up through a meadow. Mature willow trees are down by the river, younger trees are fenced. Turn left at the next junction, go down towards the river, then follow the path round to the right and up again to the two circles of trees, 'The Rings'.

④ Walk round the circles, and go down the slope towards the footbridge over the river to your right. Cross the River Colne. Turn right at Saxon Lake, a magnet for waterfowl, although it is entirely artificial, as is the Duke of Northumberland's River just behind you. It was diverted from the Colne just downstream of the last bridge, originally to power the Duke's watermills in Isleworth. Follow the path around the lake. Towards its end, opposite, concrete blocks support the banks; spaces between them are caves for bats and sand martins.

⑤ Go through the kissing gate and turn right onto the public footpath. Go through the churchyard gate, and turn half right to follow a path diagonally through it. Turn left by the church, noting Richard Cox's flat tombstone under the yew tree here (see below). Follow the path to the gate and return to the pub.

PLACES OF INTEREST NEARBY

Next to the pub, **St Mary's church** dates from the 12th century, including the decorated south doorway. The tower is not positioned squarely to the rest of the church, and is topped with an 18th century cupola. In the churchyard is buried Richard Cox, who developed Cox's Orange Pippin apples. Behind the church is Harmondsworth's famous **tithe barn**, built in 1427 when Winchester College owned the manor.

Cowley
The Crown

MAP: OS EXPLORER 172 (GR 054824)   **WALK 4**   **DISTANCE:** 3¼ MILES

DIRECTIONS TO START: THE PUB IS ON THE HIGH STREET IN COWLEY. FROM JUNCTION 4 OF THE M4 TAKE THE A408 NORTH TO COWLEY. **STATIONS:** WEST DRAYTON AND BUS 222; UNDERGROUND: UXBRIDGE (METROPOLITAN LINE) AND BUS 222. **PARKING:** THE PUB HAS A CAR PARK. ALTERNATIVELY, TRY ON-STREET PARKING EAST OF THE PUB.

Ideal for a hot summer's day, but enjoyable at any time of year, this easy walk takes you alongside two pleasant stretches of water and over a third. You start by strolling along a tree-lined section of the River Pinn, leaving it via a meadow. Moving across to the Grand Union Canal, you may meet a colourful scene of brightly painted narrowboats plying up and down the route. This attractive section of towpath is popular with boating people, walkers and anglers – whose interests are reflected in the names of the streets between the river and the canal. After reaching Cowley Lock and the lock-keeper's house you return to the pub by crossing Fray's River.

The Crown

This is a comfortable, friendly pub, popular with locals. It has a cosy traditional interior with low, beamed ceilings and on the walls are paintings and old black and white photographs of life on the canal when narrow boats were used to transport goods and materials around the country. There is a dining area adjoining the bar and the menu includes sandwiches, jacket potatoes, chilli con carne, seafood platter, sausage, eggs, bacon and chips, and steak and chips. Courage Best Bitter, Fuller's London Pride and two guest ales are on handpump.

Opening times are 12 noon to 3 pm and 5.30 pm to 11.30 pm on Monday to Saturday and 12 noon to 3 pm and 7 pm to 10.30 pm on Sunday. Food is served 12 noon to 2.30 pm and 5.30 pm to 9 pm Monday to Friday, 5.30 pm to 9 pm Saturday and 12 noon to 2.30 pm on Sunday. Children are welcome inside if they are eating, otherwise in the garden. Telephone: 01895 236415.

The Walk

① Leave the pub, turn left in the High Street and left again onto Station Road. Continue ahead when the road veers right and becomes Church Road. At St Lawrence's church on the left, bear left with the main road as it skirts the churchyard and becomes Pield Heath Road.

② Cross Robbie Bell Bridge and turn right onto a wide earth track to the left of the River Pinn. Keep on this main tree-fringed track which eventually veers left across a

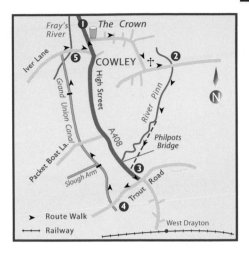

meadow. Go through a kissing gate onto Cowley High Road just south of Philpots Bridge.

③ Turn left, walk to the crossroads and turn right to cross the High Road at the lights. Go straight ahead along Trout Road. Cross the end of Gurnard Close and continue ahead, passing office and factory buildings.

④ After the First Choice Café on the left, and just before the bridge over the Grand Union Canal, take the steps on the left down to the canal towpath. Turn right onto the towpath, go under the bridge and continue ahead. Pass a two-armed London Loop signpost and continue along the towpath. Walk under the metal bridge at the Slough Arm, by a new marina. Proceed along the towpath and go through a metal kissing gate. Many narrow boats are moored on this section of the canal. Go over a hump bridge, passing the Turning Point pub on the left, and then under a stone bridge at Packet Boat Lane. Continue ahead, going under a white stone

The Grand Union Canal

bridge and eventually reaching Cowley Lock, where there is a picturesque old cottage and lock-keeper's house.

⑤ Follow the tarmac up to Iver Lane. Turn right and continue ahead, crossing the bridge over Fray's River. Turn left onto Cowley High Street and cross the road back to the Crown.

PLACES OF INTEREST NEARBY

If you have your own transport you may like to visit the **Chiltern Open Air Museum** in 45 acres of park and woodland, signposted from junction 17 of the M25. It displays 20 or more old buildings rescued from derelict areas and re-erected in an attractive Chiltern landscape, among them a blacksmith's forge, toll house, barn and stables. There is a children's adventure playground, a woodland nature trail and a tearoom. Open daily from April to October, 10 am to 5 pm. Telephone: 01494 871117. The museum is also home to the **Hawk and Owl Trust Nature Conservation Centre. Denham Country Park**, just north of the A40, is an area of diverse habitat. Colne Valley Park Visitors' Centre is within the park. Telephone: 01895 833375.

Ruislip Lido
The Waters Edge

MAP: OS EXPLORER 172 (GR 087892)   **WALK 5**   **DISTANCE:** 2½ MILES

DIRECTIONS TO START: THE PUB IS AT THE END OF RESERVOIR ROAD,
OFF DUCK HILL ROAD, THE A4180. **STATIONS:** RUISLIP (METROPOLITAN, PICCADILLY)
THEN BUS H13. **PARKING:** IN THE RESERVOIR ROAD CAR PARK NEAR THE PUB,
OR IN THE MAD BESS WOOD CAR PARK OFF DUCK HILL ROAD.

Ruislip Lido was originally established as a reservoir by the Grand Union Canal Company, and was used for bathing, boating, waterskiing and so on. The water was deemed unsafe for bathing a few years ago, and the artificial lake has become the centre of a number of attractive wildlife areas, as well as still being a good place for a family excursion. The lake is bounded by Park Wood – a shady broadleaf wood, part of an ancient oak and hornbeam forest – Poor's Field, which is of ecological interest as an area of acid heathland, and Copse Wood. The area is a haven for wildlife, from foxes to insects. In addition, Ruislip Nature Reserve, to which there is no general public access, has been created from the northern tip of the reservoir to provide open water and marshland.

The walk stays fairly close to the lake at first, then takes you across Poor's Field and into Copse Wood. This contains the site of Battle of Britain House, leased to the American secret service during the Second World War for agent training. The house burned down in 1984. Part of the route is covered by the narrow gauge railway at the Lido.

19

The Waters Edge

This pub has the perfect location. It was built on the site of the former main building of Ruislip Lido, with its lawn extending right down to the water, just like it says on the sign. The many tables and benches outside are the ideal site for a summer drink watching the lake. Perhaps a Whitbread Best Bitter or Boddingtons, or one of the lagers offered like Labatt's, Heineken or Stella. A few wines are available by the bottle. The original building, from the days when the Lido was for swimming, was apparently destroyed by fire. The pub building is quite new, and reflects the modernist style of the Lido era on the outside, and the current fashion for old-style wooden panelled rooms on the inside.

The accent is very much on eating in this family-friendly Brewers Fayre pub, with food being served from 11.30 am to 10.30 pm on Monday to Saturday and from 12 noon to 10 pm on Sunday. A complete three-course menu including daily specials and tea and coffee is available throughout the day. There is a family dining area and children's play area; meals are served only at the tables indoors. Telephone: 01895 625241.

The Walk

① Leave the pub heading south, with the Lido on your left. Follow the tarmac path round the edge, passing the green shack, and walk along the embankment. Continue round to the left at the end and pass the sandy beach, heading towards the railway.

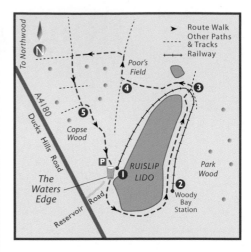

② Continue on the lakeside path to the left of Woody Bay station on the Ruislip Lido Railway, into the edge of Park Wood. Pass silver birch and beech trees, some with nesting boxes, getting glimpses of the lake through the trees. Cross a footbridge and come out of the trees into a meadow; on the right is Haste Hill station.

③ Just beyond the station, cross the narrow gauge line carefully through the pair of kissing gates. A few paces past the second gate, turn left onto a path between two fences. Go through the opening in the left hand fence into Poor's Field. Turn right onto a broad grassy path near the fence on your right, then at a fork, take the path to the half left across the field. Turn left onto a broader clearly defined track leading to the other edge of the field.

④ Turn right at the other side onto a broad straight track by the side of the wood. Just before a bridlepath marked by blue horseshoe signs on posts, turn left into Copse Wood via the wooden gate,

Poor's Field

and head west on the long straight gravel footpath with a ditch on the left. Start climbing. At a very obvious crossroads turn left onto a broad track leading uphill at first. At a junction with another path, turn right then immediately left. This path downhill has almost petered out by the time it meets the waymarked Hillingdon Trail.

⑤ Turn left here and follow the Hillingdon Trail posts, turning right at a junction, with a wire and post fence on the right. Leave the wood through the gateway, and then follow signs to the half left, joining a good gravel path leading back to the pub.

PLACES OF INTEREST NEARBY

Ruislip Lido Railway runs on weekend afternoons, and at certain times of the year during the week, from Woody Bay station by the sandy beach, to Ruislip Lido station, by the Waters Edge, and back. Check running times on 01895 622895. Originally opened in 1945, it has been expanded greatly recently. One of its attractions is *Mad Bess*, a steam locomotive built in the Ruislip Lido Railway's own workshop.

Hayes Town
The Golden Cross

DIRECTIONS TO START: THE GOLDEN CROSS PUB IS AT THE JUNCTION OF PRINTINGHOUSE LANE AND BOTWELL LANE. FROM JUNCTION 3 OF THE M4 GO NORTH ON THE A312, THEN WEST ALONG HYDE ROAD, NORTH ALONG DAWLEY ROAD AND THEN EAST ALONG BOTWELL COMMON ROAD AND BOTWELL LANE. **STATION:** HAYES & HARLINGTON, THEN WALK WEST ALONG THE GRAND UNION CANAL TOWPATH TO PRINTINGHOUSE LANE, JOINING THE CIRCULAR ROUTE AT POINT 7. **PARKING:** AT THE PUB CAR PARK OR THE CAR PARK BY THE CANAL JUST NORTH OF THE STATION.

From the pub you walk across open grassland and then along Dawley Road to Stockley Country Park. Since 1993 the London Borough of Hillingdon has planted over 14,000 native British trees here, predominantly oak, ash, hornbeam, wild cherry, hawthorn, and a variety of wildflowers. After walking through the park, with some splendid views, you return to the pub along the towpath of the Grand Union Canal.

The Golden Cross

This is a modern, large and cheery family-orientated pub. The funky interior is decorated with a hotchpotch of pictures and paraphernalia, inspired by local life both past and present – including horse saddles and brasses, aspects of canal life, football, golf and trains.

Like all pubs in the Hungry Horse chain there is a huge selection of good value dishes and a separate children's menu. Offerings tend to be meat orientated with an emphasis on steaks, but there are also fish and chicken dishes, filled jacket potatoes, salad and vegetarian options. On handpump are Ruddles County and Greene King IPA. The pub is open Monday to Saturday from 11 am to 11 pm and food is served from 12 noon to 10 pm. Sunday opening times are 12 noon to 10.30 pm and food is served from 12 noon to 9.30 pm. Telephone: 020 8573 1628.

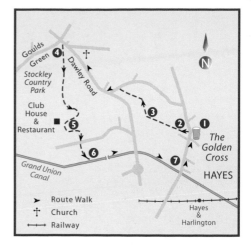

The Walk

① Exit the Golden Cross pub onto Botwell Lane. Turn left, cross the end of Printinghouse Lane and continue ahead.

② Just before the bus stop turn left through a kissing gate onto a wide earth track. Turn immediately right onto a wide grassy track. Continue straight ahead, crossing one earth track and then another.

③ To the right of a railing-topped mound, at the T-junction with another earth track, veer right. Shortly, veer left and continue ahead, passing a children's playground on the right. Continue ahead and go through

a kissing gate onto Botwell Common Road. Cross the end of this road and continue along Dawley Road. Cross the end of Princes Park Lane and further on the Ram pub on the right. Continue ahead when Dawley Road becomes Harlington Road to eventually pass the parish church of St Jerome on the right and cross the end of Judge Heath Lane.

④ Shortly, at the junction with Goulds Green on the left, and just before Harlington Road curves right, turn left and cross the road. Veer left through a metal gate into Stockley Country Park. After passing a notice board on the left continue straight ahead on a wide gravel track. Cross a footbridge, go straight over the next crosspath and proceed ahead. Ignore all turn-offs and continue along this uphill track across the golf course. Just before the brow of the hill a path veers left to a viewpoint. Back on the track continue ahead and downhill. Pass a small information board on the left and soon the golf club restaurant (open to the public) on the right.

Stockley Country Park

⑤ Shortly, at the junction of five paths do not take the obvious wide path left, but veer left on the next path around, that is a narrow downhill path between a line of trees. At the T-junction veer left, following an LL (London Loop) sign on a wooden post on the right. At the next T-junction veer right, then keep going straight ahead, following another LL sign on the left. Go ahead at a crosspaths, following another LL sign. Pass close to a fountain on the left and a two-armed LL signpost on your right. Cross over Furzeground Road and take the gravel path straight ahead, following it downhill to leave the park through a kissing gate onto the canal towpath.

⑥ Turn left, following a two-armed LL signpost to Hayes Town (1 mile). Continue ahead under an old curved brick bridge and then under Dawley Road bridge. Keep going along the towpath.

⑦ Just before the next bridge turn left through a black metal kissing gate and go ahead to Printinghouse Lane. Cross over with care and turn left, passing the Blue Anchor pub on your right. Continue ahead to return to the Golden Cross.

PLACES OF INTEREST NEARBY

The old **village centre of Hayes**, north of the Golden Cross, along Botwell Lane, is worth a stroll around. Church Walk is a pleasant cul-de-sac which borders Town Hall Park, where there is the former town hall and St Mary's church which has several features of interest.

East Bedfont
The Bell on the Green

MAP: OS EXPLORER 160 (GR 085736)   **WALK 7**   **DISTANCE:** 3 MILES

DIRECTIONS TO START: THE PUB OVERLOOKS BEDFONT GREEN ON THE SOUTH SIDE OF STAINES ROAD (A315) IN BEDFONT. **STATION:** FELTHAM AND BUS H25. **PARKING:** AT THE PUB CAR PARK OR THE CAR PARK IN BEDFONT LAKES COUNTRY PARK (POINT 3).

This is a walk for nature-lovers of all ages, exploring Bedfont Lakes Country Park, to the east of Staines. Within a short distance you will come across a number of important ecological habitats supporting a wide range of plants, birds and mammals. In addition, the grassland of the park attracts many insects, particularly butterflies. The variety of wildlife makes this a fascinating place to visit at any time of year. St Mary's church at the start of the walk is an attractive building with a wooden steeple.

The Bell on the Green

This large, welcoming pub is a friendly local and is also popular with office workers from the nearby business park at lunchtime. It's a free house with Directors and Courage Best on hand-pump and it offers a wide range of typical pub grub. There are four starters; main courses include chicken tikka masala, scampi, cod and chips, steak, roast chicken, and chicken and steak combo. Very filling sandwiches, such as steak, hot chicken, bacon and roast beef, also feature on the menu and a roast is served on Sunday. You can finish your meal with a substantial pudding. Opening times are 11.30 am to 11 pm on Monday to Saturday and 12 noon to 10.30 pm on Sunday. Telephone: 020 8751 1599.

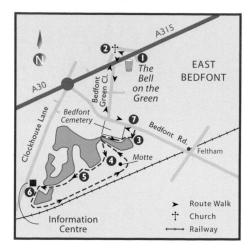

The Walk

① Leave the pub and turn left and then right to cross the busy Staines Road via the traffic island. Walk half left across the green, with a road to your right, to reach St Mary's church, Bedfont.

② With your back to the church entrance gate, cross over the road back to the green. Take the narrow tarmac path diagonally left to reach Staines Road again. Cross over with care and take the tarmac path half right across the southern section of the green. At the T-junction turn left and continue ahead on the pavement of Bedfont Green Close. When the vehicle road ends, continue on the pavement. At the T-junction turn left onto Bedfont Road, passing the cemetery on the right. After passing the bus stop, cross the road and enter Bedfont Lakes Country Park. Walk straight across the car park, through the metal barriers and ahead to Motte Lake.

③ From the bench overlooking the lake, turn left to reach the notice board. This walk takes you around the green route; details of shorter walks – red route (0.6 miles) and amber (1 mile) – are shown on the board. Facing the notice board, turn right to continue ahead. Cross a wooden bridge. At the four-ways crosspaths turn right, then almost immediately veer left onto the path up to the motte. At the fork go left, passing a picnic bench on the left. Steps here to the right lead to the top of the motte.

④ From the top take the path left and then descend the wide steps to the right. At the bottom turn left and continue along this main path that keeps near the bulge of the lake.

⑤ Just past the lifebuoy, and a bench by the rubbish bin, fork right onto a grassy

Bedfont Green and St Mary's church

track and go through a wooden gate into the nature reserve. At the fork veer left (the right fork leads to an information board which you may wish to look at). Keep on this main track, passing a bittern hide on the right. Go through another wooden gate to leave the reserve. Continue ahead, and at the T-junction turn right and continue along this main path which now skirts the east side of South Lake. At the fork bear right to visit the information centre.

⑥ Leave the information centre and walk ahead to the wide pebbled driveway. Turn right and then left to go through the metal barrier. Go ahead on the path to the fishing lake. At the T-junction go right. Continue ahead with the lake on the left and, soon, the railway line on the right. At the fork go right, away from the lake, and continue on the main path which stays close to the

railway line for some time. Take the next turning right and keep on this path which runs close to the railway line again. Keep on this main path that eventually curves left and then right, and passes the motte on the left. At the crossroads continue ahead, cross the wooden bridge and continue through the car park onto Bedfont Road.

⑦ Return to the pub by retracing your steps to the green: turn left onto Bedfont Road, cross over, turn right onto Bedfont Green Close and veer left onto the tarmac track back to the pub.

PLACES OF INTEREST NEARBY
The information centre at **Bedfont Lakes Country Park**, passed on the walk, is open every day except Christmas Day from 8 am to dusk or 9 pm, whichever is earlier. Telephone; 01784 423556.

Hatton & Hounslow Heath
The Green Man

MAP: OS EXPLORER 161 (GR 103752) • **WALK 8** • **DISTANCE:** 4 MILES

DIRECTIONS TO START: TAKE THE A312 NORTH AND CONTINUE NORTH-WEST ON FAGGS ROAD. THE GREEN MAN IS ON THE RIGHT AT THE JUNCTION WITH GREEN MAN LANE, JUST SOUTH OF THE A30. **UNDERGROUND:** HATTON CROSS (PICCADILLY LINE). **PARKING:** AT THE PUB CAR PARK OR USE THE CAR PARK IN STAINES ROAD AND START THE WALK AT POINT 3.

This walk goes through attractive woodland by the River Crane – a route used by the donkeys that used to carry materials to gunpowder mills in Brazil Mill Wood – and part of Hounslow Heath. Once a forest where Norman kings hunted, the heath later became a military training field used by Oliver Cromwell and a First World War airfield. From 1919 to 1920 it held London's first civil airport, where the world's first scheduled air service took off for Paris. After years of gravel-quarrying, the heath became a Local Nature Reserve in 1991. On both the outward and return route you cross the Duke of Northumberland's River, which was once used to power the gunpowder mills. Finally, you retrace your steps to the pub along the river path through Donkey Wood.

The Green Man

Situated at the end of a quiet lane overlooking a village green, the Green Man is an unexpected delight, resembling a pub in a rural idyll. The interior lives up to this promise, with low-beamed ceilings, secluded nooks and crannies and, in winter, roaring open fires. The public bar has a huge fireplace which, legend claims, once concealed a hiding place for highwaymen. During alterations a sooty cavity was uncovered containing a number of small objects, including clay pipes. A section was kept exposed and can now be viewed through glass.

The Green Man is a Scottish and Newcastle house and has Courage Best on handpump, also a good range of bottled lagers and wines. There is a large garden – dogs welcome – and a children's play area; children are also welcome in the pub. Tasty homecooked food, including vegetarian dishes, is served every day from 12 noon to 9.30 pm. On Sunday a traditional roast is offered from 12 noon to 5 pm. Opening times are Monday to Saturday 11 am to 11 pm and Sunday 12 noon to 10.30 pm. Telephone: 020 8890 2681.

The Walk

① Leave the pub and turn left onto Green Man Lane. Continue ahead to the T-junction and turn left onto The Causeway. Continue ahead passing a lake on the left.

② Just before the bridge over the River Crane turn left through a metal kissing gate and descend steps to the river. Turn right and go under the bridge to enter

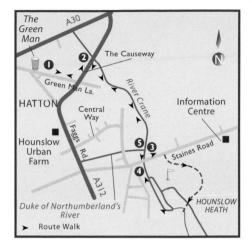

Donkey Wood, part of the River Crane Park. Continue ahead along the right river bank, go through a metal kissing gate and proceed along a wooden walkway. At the end of the walkway keep going on this main path which eventually veers right to cross a wooden bridge. Keep ahead, and cross another wooden bridge. These bridges are at the confluence of the River Crane and Duke of Northumberland's River. Turn left and continue ahead passing a yellow arrow on a wooden post. Exit onto Staines Road through a green metal barrier. Turn left on Staines Road and continue ahead across the bridge over the Crane.

③ Turn right, crossing Staines Road with care, to enter Hounslow Heath Golf Course. Continue straight ahead on the tarmac passing the club house on the left. Continue ahead on a wide earth track, at first going slightly uphill across the golf course. Carry on when it levels out, ignoring a track veering right downhill. Go slightly downhill, still on the main track, and veer right with it. Keep going, passing 'Tee 7' on a red sign on the left. Cross a

The River Crane in Brazil Mill Wood

bridge over the Crane, which at this point is split in two. Continue straight ahead, ignoring a path veering left, and one turning right to run by the river. Go through a metal barrier and cross a metal bridge over the other branch of the river. Turn right to enter Brazil Mill Wood and continue ahead on the path closest to the river. Keep going, crossing a wooden footbridge over a ditch but ignoring a footbridge over the river, on the right.

④ Just before Staines Road bridge follow the path as it veers left, and leave Brazil Mill Wood through the green metal barrier. Turn right to reach Staines Road. Cross over with care and turn right then left to re-enter Donkey Wood at the point where you left it earlier in the walk. Continue ahead along the path. Turn right

across the bridge and go ahead across the second bridge.

⑤ Stay on the path veering left. Keep close to the river and when you exit the wood at The Causeway turn right, then right again onto Green Lane and back to the pub.

PLACES OF INTEREST NEARBY

Hounslow Heath Nature Trail starts at the information centre in the north-east corner of the reserve. Telephone: 0208 577 3664. There is a car park near the centre. **Hounslow Urban Farm** – on Faggs Road next to Hatton Cemetery – is a rare-breeds centre with a café, toilets, picnic area and play area. Open (admission charge) on Tuesday to Sunday and bank holidays, 10 am to 4 pm; closed from 1 November to 31 January. Telephone: 020 8751 0850.

Cranford
The Crane

DIRECTIONS TO START: THE PUB IS ON HYDE ROAD. FROM JUNCTION 3 OF THE
M4 TAKE THE A312 NORTH AND HYDE ROAD IS THE FIRST TURNING LEFT.
STATION: HAYES & HARLINGTON. **PARKING:** THE PUB CAR PARK. THERE IS ALSO
A CAR PARK IN CRANFORD PARK NEAR ST DUNSTAN'S CHURCH (START AT POINT 4).

This pleasant stroll explores Cranford Countryside Park, in which meadows, woodlands, hedgerows and wetlands together support a wide diversity of wildflowers and birdlife. All that remains of Cranford Manor House (of which this was once the grounds) are the arch of the stable block, the ha-ha (a ditch which separated the gardens from the grazing lands), the wall of a walled garden and the 16th century church, St Dunstan's. Woodlands, planted in the 19th century, have areas of larch, ash, hornbeam, Scots pine and giant redwood.

The Crane

This typical city pub is furnished traditionally and is welcoming and comfortable, with dark wood-panelled walls, dark wood tables and upholstered chairs. A Scottish and Newcastle house, it has Courage Best on handpump. Tasty pub grub favourites are served, such as filled jacket potatoes, burgers, all-day breakfast, steak pie and mixed grill, and a roast is offered on Sunday. A range of filled rolls is also available. The pub has a garden (where dogs are welcome) and children's play area. The bar is open all day for drinks and food is served from 11 am to 9.30 pm on Monday to Saturday and 12 noon to 9 pm on Sunday. Telephone: 020 8573 2103.

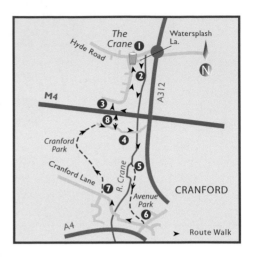

The Walk

① Exit the pub and turn right and right again onto Watersplash Lane. Turn left and then right, to the right of a wide green metal gate, into Cranford Park. After passing an information board on the right, head half left across the grass to another information board.

② Don't cross the bridge behind the information board but, following an HT (Hillingdon Trail) sign, continue ahead on the path to the right of the River Crane. Keep on this main path as it veers right and then left, and then, just beyond a white arrow on the left, enters woodland. The path then veers right to run parallel and to the right of the M4.

③ At the T-junction of paths turn left to go through St Dunstan's subway under the M4. Continue through the archway of a stable block and proceed ahead. At the beginning of a metal fence on the right, turn left through a green metal kissing gate. Turn right and then right again to enter the information centre. To continue the walk retrace your steps through the green kissing gate to pass St Dunstan's church on the left. Veer right with the wide tarmac road passing a car park on the right.

④ Turn right through a gap between a wooden gate on the right and a fence on the left. Turn left and walk across the grass to the right of a line of trees and the fence. Turn right with the path when you reach the river and walk along its right bank. Continue along this path, which is soon flanked by shrubbery. When the shrubbery on the right ends, proceed ahead and shortly cross a bridge over the river to Avenue Park.

⑤ Turn right and follow a grassy path to the left of a stretch of grass and the tree-lined river. Keep going ahead, then when the expanse of grassland narrows, and just before three young sycamore trees, veer

Cranford Countryside Park

right with the main path, and then veer left. Keep going on this main track, soon veering left again and then right. The river is to your right and there is grassland to your left. After you pass playing fields on the left, veer left with the path, passing a plantation of saplings on the right.

⑥ At the end of the plantation turn right with the path and follow it to the end at Cranford Lane. Turn right and continue ahead to cross Cranford Bridge, taking care as there is no pavement. Pass a 'Welcome to Harlington' sign on the left and continue ahead.

⑦ Opposite the end of Langley Crescent, at a green metal barrier, turn right to re-enter Cranford Park. Turn left through a wooden gate and continue ahead. Veer right with the path when you reach the trees. Continue ahead on this main path which has HT markers. At a narrow gap in the trees on the left, turn left, following the

HT arrow to go through wooden barriers. Continue ahead on this tree-lined main path. Keep on when it veers right, following an HT sign, then veer left through a wide gap in a wall, the remains of a walled garden. Continue ahead until you reach the stable block arch and St Dunstan's subway again.

⑧ Turn left under the subway and go straight ahead to Roseville Road and turn right onto it. Veer left with the road and continue ahead to the pub at the end on the right.

PLACES OF INTEREST NEARBY
Heathrow Airport Visitor Centre, off the Northern Perimeter Road (follow signs), gives you a peep behind the scenes at the world's busiest international airport, with interactive displays, a Boeing 777 cockpit mock-up and worksheets for children. Open daily from 10 am to 5 pm. Entry is free. Telephone: 020 8745 6655.

Norwood Green
The Plough

DIRECTIONS TO START: THE PUB IS AT 10 TENTELOW LANE, OFF NORWOOD ROAD, THE A3005. **STATION:** SOUTHALL (SUBURBAN RAIL), THEN 120 BUS TO THE GREEN. BUS E5 GOES NEXT TO THE CANAL IN POINT 2. **PARKING:** THERE IS A SMALL FREE CAR PARK NEXT TO THE PUB, OPPOSITE THE CHURCH.

Norwood Green is a giant village green in a semi-rural area cut off from the rest of Southall by the canal and the M4. Just off the green is a picturesque church, dating back to the 12th or 13th century, but looking mostly Victorian, and the village pub. This attractive stroll takes you first through a wood off Tentelow Lane, part of which is council-owned as part of a wildlife habitat strategy. Most of the walk is along the towpath of the Grand Union Canal, starting with Three Bridges, an ingenious structure from 1856 by Brunel, possibly his last design. A road crosses the canal which itself crosses the railway line (the towpath counts as a separate bridge). Glade Lane Countryside Park, which you see next, features an old hay meadow not cut until autumn to allow flowering plants to seed. The towpath leads you past locks and scenes of canal life, back to the green.

The Plough

This is the oldest pub in Southall, a wonderful building dating back over 600 years, with low ceilings, exposed beams and traditional decorations like horse brasses. There is a cosy small bar with tables and settles, plus a larger dining area. This is a pub that is very much at the centre of village life, with its busy notice board reminding regulars of local events. It is a Fuller's pub, with London Pride, Chiswick Bitter and ESB on handpump.

Food is served at lunchtime and in the evening until about 9 pm (but no chips in the evening). For lunch the kitchen swiftly turns out traditional pub favourites, such as ham and eggs, burgers, pies, sausages and omelettes, accompanied by home-made chips and salad or vegetables. Delicious-looking filled rolls, desserts and tea or coffee are also available. The Plough has a large garden surrounded by trees, and a children's play area. Telephone: 020 8574 1945.

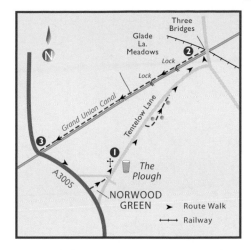

The Walk

① Coming out of the pub, turn right onto Tentelow Lane and pass the bowling club. Just before the first roundabout, at Minterne Avenue, turn right through a kissing gate and follow the public footpath diagonally across the field to the wood. Enter the small broadleaf wood, which is good for blackberrying, and take the left fork, staying in the wood between Tentelow Lane on the left and the sports ground. The floor is carpeted with acorns in the autumn, and the occasional oak has been fitted with a nesting box. Leave the wood

to the left at the sports club, walking through their car park, then turn right on Tentelow Lane. At the roundabout, turn left onto Windmill Lane.

St Mary's church, Norwood Green

Hanwell Lock

② Cross the canal and railway line via Three Bridges. Cross to the right hand side of the bridge, then walk down to the towpath and come back under the bridge on the towpath, heading towards the Paddington Arm and Southall. Pass a sign reading 'Braunston 90 miles', and then pass Glade Lane Meadow. Pass the lock, go under the bridge and pass Norwood Top Lock and cottage. Go through a kissing gate and walk past long-term moorings on the opposite bank. Continue over a humpback bridge at the entrance to a dock, which led to factories, including the former Monsted margarine works. Then go under a footbridge, staying on the towpath.

③ At the next road bridge, climb the steps to Norwood Road, turn left and cross the canal. Pass an appropriate pair of pubs: the Lamb on the left and then the Wolf on the right. Walk a little way down the green, then turn left and walk across it, passing St Mary's church to return to the pub.

PLACES OF INTEREST NEARBY
Osterley Park is a treasure of the National Trust, featuring what is originally a 16th century merchant's house (admission fee) greatly altered in the 18th century to the designs of Robert Adam. The grounds are extensive, and a café and a shop are provided. There is a pay car park. From Norwood Green, walk down Osterley Lane, or drive down Norwood Road/Heston Road and follow the boundary of the property.

Bentley Priory
The Case is Altered

DIRECTIONS TO START: TURN WESTWARDS OFF THE A409 AT HARROW WEALD COMMON. THE PUB IS ON THE SOUTH SIDE OF OLD REDDING, NEXT TO THE VIEWPOINT. **STATIONS:** STANMORE (JUBILEE) OR HATCH END (SUBURBAN RAIL) THEN BUS H12 ALONG UXBRIDGE ROAD AND BUS 258 UP BROOKSHILL. **PARKING:** IN THE PUBLIC CAR PARK ON OLD REDDING NEXT TO THE PUB, FOR THE VIEW!

Bentley Priory is a secure MOD site; the RAF ran much of the Battle of Britain from it. The core of the house was designed by John Soane, but you can't see it. The grounds form a Local Nature Reserve, however, which you really must see. It is a managed Site of Special Scientific Interest including woodland, scrub, grassland, streams, a lake and a fenced-in deer park. It provides habitats for a great variety of wildlife, and is a good place for birdwatchers. The walk also takes you through part of Harrow Weald Common. Its woods include oak, silver birch and beech.

The Case is Altered

One theory about the puzzling name of this long-established popular pub on Old Redding is that it is a corruption of Casa Alta, the Spanish for 'high house'. Gradually enlarged over the years, the Case is Altered has a couple of welcoming bars with tables indoors, and a large garden with a children's play area. Currently food is only available at lunchtime, from 12 noon until 2 pm, Tuesday to Sunday, but check this before coming. The choice ranges from baguettes and jacket potatoes to steak pie or lasagne, standard pub dishes but you can have a delicious three-course meal, rounded off with sticky toffee pudding, spotted dick or fudge cakes. Morland Old Speckled Hen, Burton and Bass beers are handpumped. The pub is open all day in summer; in winter (roughly September to March) it is closed from 3 pm to 5.30 pm. Telephone: 020 8954 1002.

The Walk

NB: Be prepared for some muddy patches in the nature reserve and on the common.

① Leaving the pub, turn right and then right again down the track to Copse Farm. Pass White Cottage, keep left of Copse Farm, then turn left onto a public footpath signposted to Brookshill, along Brookshill Drive. At the end of the drive, turn right and walk downhill just over 50 paces, then before the bend in the road, cross over and turn left onto the public footpath signposted 'Clamp Hill' and 'Circular Walk'. Follow the path alongside the hedge and wild shrubbery. At the end, cross Clamp Hill and turn right, then left into the first drive, following the signs for Lower Priory Farm and the public footpath. Before the gate into the livery yard, take the public footpath to the half right, signposted 'Stanmore Hill'. Follow the path by the stream on your left, with fields behind it, and woods on the right.

② At the end of a road with housing, Masefield Avenue, turn left through a metal gate into Bentley Priory Local Nature Reserve. Follow a path to the left of the map of the reserve facing you. Keep the fenced-off wood close on your right. Turn right onto another path, still with the fence on your right. Continue to a large clearing in the wood on your left. Ahead, beyond the fence, is an apparent fire-break in the wood. Go through the gap in the fence, or the kissing gate to the left, keep straight on, and turn left onto a metalled path leading through the wood. Go through a kissing gate by a five-bar gate, and walk past the fenced deer park on the right. The woods on the left include hornbeams.

③ Turn left at a tarmac path signposted 'Harrow Weald Common', by another map

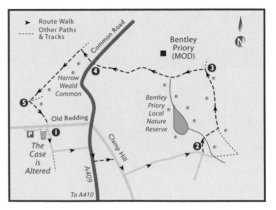

The pub's attractive garden

of the reserve. This gives you a view of Bentley Priory to the right, or its clocktower at least. The concrete path snakes through the wood of small trees and shrubs, occasionally giving you a good view to the left. Follow a yellow arrow through a wooden kissing gate, and go along a virtual tunnel of foliage, by the fence on the left, then between two fences. Go through a five-barred gate onto Common Road.

④ Cross the road with care; take the public footpath opposite to 'Harrow Weald Common', down steps into the wood, following yellow arrows on stakes downhill. Cross another path, continuing away from the road, and turn left onto another path going from right to left near the edge of the wood. Keep by the edge of the wood, crossing a few streams. Pass a track to the right, then on the left the end of an avenue

of trees, 'Len's Avenue', planted by Leonard Renery, a Keeper of the Common for over 30 years, whose ashes were scattered here.

⑤ Pass Grimsdyke Cottages on the right. Follow the yellow arrow to the left, then take the fork to the half right, not the bridleway marked with white posts. Continue on this broad track down to the gate. Go onto Old Redding and turn right to return to the pub. Make sure that you see the view from the car park.

> ### PLACES OF INTEREST NEARBY
> The **two churches of St John** in Stanmore, eastwards along Uxbridge Road (A410), are worth seeing. One, from the beginning of the 17th century, is now a picturesque ruin, having been supplanted by the 19th century building of stone. W. S. Gilbert is buried in the churchyard.

Harrow
The Castle

DIRECTIONS TO START: HARROW IS REACHED VIA THE A4005 (HARROW ROAD/SUDBURY HILL/LONDON ROAD). THE PUB IS AT THE JUNCTION OF WEST STREET AND CROWN STREET. **STATIONS:** HARROW ON THE HILL (METROPOLITAN), NEAR POINT 5; SUDBURY HILL (PICCADILLY), NEAR POINT 4. **PARKING:** THE PUB HAS NO CAR PARK. THERE IS SOME ON-STREET PARKING NEARBY BUT TRAFFIC IS DISCOURAGED FROM THE OLD CENTRE OF HARROW. THERE ARE PAY CAR PARKS NORTH OF HARROW ON THE HILL STATION.

Think 'Harrow' and you think of the famous school, but another feature of Harrow is a number of private estates with their own woods and paddocks, which gives them a country atmosphere. This stroll provides a taste of these, and some of the grand houses on Sudbury Hill and London Road, before taking you through the centre of Harrow, with a fascinating mix of private and school buildings, and to the church of Harrow on the Hill with its view that inspired Byron.

The Castle

This is a friendly Fuller's pub, with a public bar at the front, and a saloon bar reached down the side passageway, which has tables, chairs and gas heaters for al fresco patrons. The saloon bar is carpeted and has a real fireplace and proper wooden bar. There is also a back room for dining, and a garden in summer. Since this is Harrow, in the public bar you may overhear conversations that take in student grant policies and the qualities of dry sherries.

Food is served from 12 noon to 2.30 pm (or a bit later), and from 6 pm to 9 pm. The food is made with care, and ranges from delicious, freshly-prepared sandwiches, like Stilton and apple, through calamari nibbles, to pub grub favourites and some enticing daily specials listed on a board. Desserts are also available. Fuller's London Pride, Chiswick Bitter and ESB are served, together with a seasonal ale, such as Summer Ale or Red Fox. Telephone: 020 8422 3155.

The Walk

① Leave the pub and turn left down Crown Street. Turn left into Byron Hill Road, then right into West Hill. Pass West Hill Hall, go down the alley and turn left to go up Roxeth Hill. Cross and go up the right hand side.

② Turn right at the top into London Road. Turn right into Mount Park Avenue, then left into Mount Park Road. Just past the sixth form college, Duneaves was the home of R. M. Ballantyne, the 19th century author of dozens of adventure

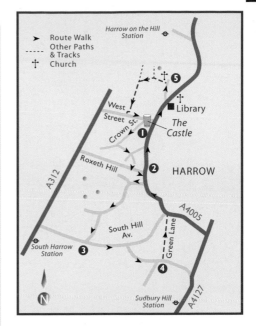

stories. Continue downhill, passing a house that is a converted 19th century billiard room. Past Ingleby Road turn left – do not continue along the west spur of Mount Park Avenue. Walk down to the toll gate at the end.

③ Turn left and pass the toll gate on South Hill Avenue. The road passes through the site of Orley Farm School; part of the grounds on the right is ancient woodland. Pass by the playing field on the left, also bordered by woods, then turn right onto Orley Farm Road. Follow this round to the left, pass the end of Hill Close, and pass more toll gates.

④ Turn left onto the tree-lined bridleway uphill, Green Lane. It is signposted to Sudbury Hill, and has a sports ground on the right. At the top, cross South Hill Avenue, and continue uphill on the main road, Sudbury Hill, becoming London

Church Hill, Harrow

Road. Cross to the right hand side. Keep straight on as it enters Harrow on the Hill; do not follow the main road down Roxeth Hill. After The Square (really a triangle), continue along High Street, getting a view of the church on the hilltop. Pass school outfitters, cafés, the Headmaster's house, and opposite the Vaughan Library, fork left up Church Hill passing the School Chapel on the right and the Old Schools on the left.

⑤ Enter St Mary's churchyard. There has been a church on this site since 1094, but the building now looks Victorian because of renovations carried out by George Gilbert Scott (who also built the library and chapel). John Lyon, the founder of Harrow School, is buried inside. Byron's daughter Allegra is buried near the porch. Follow the path through the churchyard.

The Peachey gravestone, on which Byron reputedly lay, writing poetry, is now enclosed in railings. You can still admire the view. Walk down the footpath by the churchyard, following the sign to Bessborough Road. The path ends at the top of a sloping meadow. Walk down towards a row of poplars, and turn left onto a tarmac path. Keep on the broader path, and at the end, follow it through the houses and turn left onto West Street, following it uphill back to the pub.

PLACES OF INTEREST NEARBY
The **Old Speech Room Gallery** in Church Hill contains the original Old Schools part of Harrow School, and has public art exhibitions. It is open from 2.30 pm to 5.30 pm, not Wednesdays, during term time. Telephone: 020 8872 8205/8000.

Horsenden Hill
The Ballot Box

MAP: OS EXPLORER 173 (GR 159847) | **WALK 13** | **DISTANCE:** 2¼ MILES

DIRECTIONS TO START: THE BALLOT BOX PUB IS ON THE EAST SIDE OF HORSENDEN LANE NORTH. EITHER TAKE THE A4127 NORTH AND TURN RIGHT JUST BEFORE THE A4090, OR GO WEST ON THE A4090 FROM THE WEMBLEY DIRECTION AND TURN LEFT ONTO MELVILLE AVENUE, THE NORTHERN CONTINUATION OF HORSENDEN LANE NORTH. **STATIONS:** GREENFORD IS CLOSE TO POINT 6 ON THE WALK; UNDERGROUND: PERIVALE OR GREENFORD (CENTRAL LINE) OR SUDBURY HILL (PICCADILLY LINE). **PARKING:** AT THE PUB OR USE THE CAR PARK ON HORSENDEN HILL AND START THE WALK AT POINT 3.

The walk begins with a gradual climb through superb ancient woodland to Horsenden Hill, an area of outstanding natural beauty. Look out for housemartins, swallows, green woodpeckers, skylarks, meadow pipits, wagtails, warblers and finches. On clear days there are views over five counties and ten London boroughs. Wildflowers along the way in season include lesser celandine, purple bugle and cuckoo flower. You then stroll along a rural-seeming section of the Paddington Arm of the Grand Union Canal and return through meadows to the pub.

The Ballot Box

This relaxed, family-friendly pub has a large, comfortably furnished, open-plan interior and a garden. Its forerunner, demolished during the Second World War to make way for an artillery gun, got its name in the 19th century when boat people used to walk from the canal to vote at the inn.

The Ballot Box's large and varied menu includes cauliflower and sun dried tomatoes au gratin and chicken florentine pasta, as well as pub favourites such as mixed grill, steak and ale pie and fish and chips, all in generous helpings. On handpump are Tetley Bitter, Bass Bitter and Blackthorn cider. Opening times are 11 am to 11 pm on Monday to Saturday and 12 noon to 10.30 pm on Sunday. Food is served from 12 noon to 10 pm on Monday to Friday and 12 noon to 9 pm on Saturday and Sunday. Children are allowed in the pub and garden, which has an outdoor play area and an excellent Wacky Warehouse that they may be reluctant to leave for a walk. Telephone: 020 8902 2825.

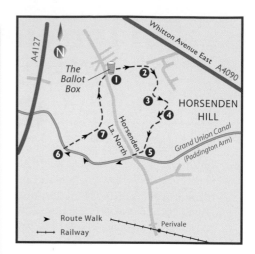

The Walk

① Leaving the pub, turn right on Horsenden Lane North, and almost immediately turn right onto a narrow tarmac path to enter Horsenden Hill, passing a notice board on the left.

② When you reach a crosspaths, just before the end of the houses of Whitton Drive, turn right and at the fork keep right to enter Horsenden Wood. Pass a post with a white arrow on the left. Eventually you'll pass a large circular fenced-off enclosure of young trees on the right. Veer right here and you'll shortly reach a T-junction.

③ Turn left at the junction. Cross a tarmac crosspath and, passing the car park on your right, continue uphill in woodland. Keep on the path when it veers slightly right to leave the woodland and level out. Continue across a meadow towards a fence, passing a white arrow on a post on the left. Between the arrow and the fence look for a concrete obelisk, an OS triangulation point. Turn left and walk to the obelisk. Then veer left, aiming for the point where the line of shrubbery and trees ahead of you turns right, and there are three trees close together and a golf tee beyond, to the left. Walk between these three trees and this point and continue ahead, keeping close to the shrubbery, then veering left with it. Pass a flight of descending wooden steps on the right. At the end of the line of trees and shrubs, veer right, turn immediately left onto a tarmac track and stop just short of the golf course to admire the view.

④ To leave, turn around and walk straight ahead on the tarmac. Pass the flight of

Horsenden Hill

wooden steps, now ascending, on your right. Keep on this main path downhill and pass a fenced-off meadow planted with wildflowers, some now rare. At the end of the meadow turn right on a wide dirt track. Stay on this main path as it veers right and slightly downhill. At a crosspaths continue ahead and at the T-junction turn left. Continue downhill to the path's end at Horsenden Lane North.

(5) Turn left and pass the entrance to Horsenden Farm. Cross the bridge over the canal and turn left down the steps, then turn left on the towpath, go under the bridge and continue ahead.

(6) Go under a graceful arched footbridge, turn left through a metal kissing gate and go ahead up a metal path. Turn left, cross the canal bridge and follow the metal path when it turns right. Go through a kissing gate onto the western section of Horsenden Hill. Ahead is an information board.

(7) Turn left and go ahead, soon passing a playing field on the left. Veer slightly left through a gap in the trees that form the top periphery of the field. Cross a wooden footbridge over a ditch into a smaller playing field. Continue ahead and veer slightly right to go through a wide gap in the far right corner of the field. Turn right to reach Horsenden Lane North and cross over, back to the pub.

PLACES OF INTEREST NEARBY

London Motorcycle Museum, at Ravenor Park, Oldfield Lane South, Greenford, is the only one of its kind in the city. The exhibits include a Brough Superior seen in *Dad's Army* and enthusiasts wanting advice on restoration are welcome. Open on Saturday and Sunday and bank holidays, 10 am to 4.30 pm. Admission is free. Telephone: 020 8575 6644.

Hanwell
The Fox

DIRECTIONS TO START: THE PUB IS AT THE END OF GREEN LANE, OLD HANWELL. FROM UXBRIDGE ROAD (A4020) IN HANWELL, TURN SOUTH ONTO LOWER BOSTON ROAD AND THEN ONTO GREEN LANE. **STATION:** HANWELL (NEAR POINT 7). **PARKING:** ROADSIDE OR USE THE CAR PARK AT CHURCHFIELDS RECREATION GROUND AND START THE WALK AT POINT 6.

Starting near the Hanwell flight of locks on the Grand Union Canal, this walk offers a wonderful mixture of wildlife and 19th century architecture. You'll share the River Brent's waterside path, among trees and wildflowers, with many species of birds and waterfowl. The route passes the impressive Wharncliffe rail viaduct, built in 1838 by Brunel to carry the main railway line; its hollow brick piers are now home to colonies of bats. Does St Mary's church, towards the end of the walk, have a familiar look? It was built by Sir George Gilbert Scott, the architect of St Pancras station (as well as Harrow School library and chapel – see Walk 12).

The Fox

Well situated at the end of a quiet cul-de-sac near the Grand Union Canal's Hanwell flight of locks, the Fox dates back to the early 1800s. Convivial and attractive it has a public bar near the entrance and a dining area at the back. There's also a large garden.

The Fox is a freehouse; beers on handpump are Fuller's London Pride, Timothy Taylor's, Brakspear Bitter and frequent guest ales. The food is imaginative and varied. Offerings are chalked up on a board and change daily, for example trout and almonds, grilled salmon and lamb with rosemary, all served with well-prepared fresh vegetables. There are always at least two vegetarian dishes available. Children and dogs are welcome. Telephone: 020 8567 4021 or 020 8567 3912.

The Walk

① From the pub turn left and continue ahead. Turn right at the canal towpath and pass the first lock of the Hanwell flight. Veer right to follow a Brent River Park (BRP) arrow on a wooden post. Continue along this path to the left of the river. At the fork veer right and follow the path under the Uxbridge Road bridge. Follow the path by the Brent towards the Wharncliffe rail viaduct.

② Cross the river by the bridge at the viaduct, then turn left and go under the viaduct. Go through the wooden kissing gate into the park and turn left, following another BRP arrow. At the T-junction veer left onto the path around the perimeter of the park. Go through a double metal

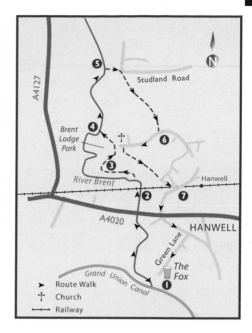

kissing gate to enter Brent Lodge Park. Continue ahead, passing some animal enclosures. At the entrance to the Millennium Maze turn right with the wide tarmac track. Pass between a playground on the left and a café on the right to reach the animal centre.

③ With your back to the entrance to the animal centre, take the tarmac path ahead to the end of the animal enclosure. Do not turn right with the tarmac path but strike out across the grass, veering only slightly right. Go downhill to the river bank and turn right to walk along it. Staying near the river, keep on this path as it curves right. Go down wooden steps and through a kissing gate. Turn left, then left again to cross a bridge over the river.

④ Turn right following a BRP arrow. Continue ahead and at the fork veer right to keep near the river. At the T-junction

The path through Rest Garden

turn right to continue along the left river bank. At the fork, veer left to continue ahead, passing a bridge on the right. When the path ends, veer right over the grass and continue ahead still by the river, now flanked by Brent Valley golf course.

⑤ Cross the next bridge and walk straight ahead across the grass towards the end of the row of houses on Studland Road. Just short of the houses go up the incline and turn right on a wide track. Follow the track to its end at Church Road.

⑥ Turn right, cross the road and continue in the same direction on the pavement. When the pavement ends, continue ahead on the tarmac path to the left of Church Road along the perimeter of Churchfields Recreation Ground. Continue on this path when it turns left short of a car park and opposite St Mary's church, Hanwell. Continue on the path through the park, between chestnut trees. After passing the end of Manor Court Road, pass between three metal posts onto Alwyne Road. Walk along the pavement and turn right under the viaduct.

⑦ Ignore the path immediately right but take the next right through a green metal gate into the well-kept Rest Garden. Descend the steps, turn right and then left to walk along the tarmac path by the left side of the pond. Leave the park at the end of Half Acre Road. Walk ahead along this road and turn right at the T-junction onto Uxbridge Road. At the lights by the Viaduct pub, cross the central reservation at the end of Lower Boston Road. Turn right to cross over, then left to walk along the right side of the road. Turn right onto Green Lane and continue to the pub.

PLACES OF INTEREST NEARBY
The **small zoo in Brent Lodge Park** is a delight for children. Outdoor enclosures (free) contain rabbits, guinea pigs and birds and an animal centre houses a variety of small mammals. It is usually open during daylight hours. There is a nominal entry fee. Telephone: 020 8758 5916.

Twickenham
The White Swan

MAP: OS EXPLORER (GR 165733)   **WALK 15**   **DISTANCE:** 3 MILES

DIRECTIONS TO START: THE PUB IS ON RIVERSIDE. FROM RICHMOND ROAD (A305) TURN SOUTH ONTO SION ROAD TO REACH RIVERSIDE.
STATION: TWICKENHAM. **PARKING:** NONE AT THE PUB, BUT THERE IS A PUBLIC CAR PARK BY THE RIVER WEST OF THE PUB.

Twickenham, where the walk begins, is a London riverside village with a distinctive nautical feel. Some of its historic mansions are open to the public. This walk, after a stroll along an attractive section of the Thames towpath, explores the grounds of two beautiful 18th century houses: Marble Hill House (a magnificent villa in the Palladian style, beloved by admirers of the Italian architect Palladio) and York House, where the outdoor vistas include a fountain complete with voluptuous stone nymphs, and a sculpture garden.

The White Swan

An atmospheric 17th century pub, the White Swan has bare floorboards, wood benches and open fireplaces. Outside is a terrace and, across the road, benches by the river. Beers on handpump are Marston's Pedigree, Charles Wells Bombardier, Shepherd Neame Spitfire, Greene King IPA and at least one guest beer. There is also a good selection of wines and bottled lagers. With loads of rugby memorabilia on display, this becomes a place for fans on match days – recalling the revelry it hosted when this was a staging post for coaches.

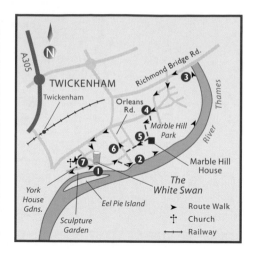

There is a cold buffet daily from April to October, and weekend barbecues from May to September. A typical winter menu might include soup, beer-battered cod and chips, liver with mash and bacon, sandwiches and Sunday roasts, plus vegetarian dishes. Children and dogs are welcome. The bar is open all day in summer, and in winter from 11 am to 3 pm and 5.30 pm to 11 pm on Monday to Thursday, 11 am to 11 pm on Friday and Saturday and 12 noon to 10.30 pm on Sunday. Telephone: 020 8892 2166.

The Walk

① Leave the pub and turn left to walk along Riverside. Cross the end of a road called Lebanon Park and continue ahead. Follow the road as it curves right to skirt the grounds of Orleans House.

② Opposite four steps up to a wooden door to Orleans House, turn right onto a tarmac path and keep on it when it veers left to run by the river. Pass a playground on the left and go ahead between wide gateposts to continue along the riverside road. After passing the quay for the ferry to Ham and Marble Hill Park on the left, continue ahead on the Thames Path towards Richmond Bridge.

③ At Richmond Bridge follow the path left and away from the river onto Richmond Bridge Road. Continue as far as Morley Road and turn left. Turn right onto Alexandra Road and left onto Cambridge Park (a road). Veer first right, following a sign 'Cambridge Park nos 1-14', then turn right at the T-junction. Still on Cambridge Park cross over and then cross the end of Beaufort Road.

④ Turn left through a wooden gate into Marble Hill Park. Veer right, then turn right at the T-junction to walk on a path parallel to the road. Opposite a path veering right to leave the park, turn left and walk across the grass to Marble Hill House. The visitors' entrance is on the left.

⑤ To continue the walk, with your back to

the house, turn left and walk on the tarmac path skirting the curved wall on your left. At the end of the wall turn left, continue along the curved tarmac and turn left again to view the front of the house. Return to the end of the curved wall, passing on your left a signpost to the Coachhouse and Toilets. At the T-junction turn left and, passing a two-armed sign, follow it to the Coachhouse and Toilets. Pass the end of the Coachhouse building on your right and a rugby field on your left. Continue ahead on the tarmac track and through a wooden gate onto Orleans Road.

⑥ Turn right, continue ahead and turn left onto Richmond Road. Go ahead passing Orleans Park School on the left. Turn left onto Lebanon Park following a sign for Orleans House Gallery. Take the first right, still on Lebanon Park, and continue ahead. Cross over Sion Road and veer slightly left to go through the wrought iron gates into the gardens of York House. Take the first left and continue ahead on a pebble path which veers right. At the T-junction veer right and at the next T-junction turn right. After crossing a wooden bridge over a pond, turn left and ascend eight brick steps to go through an archway. Continue ahead, passing York House on the right.

⑦ Climb the steps on the left to cross the bridge over Riverside. At a circular pond veer right and go through a gap in the hedge. Walk across the grass to a fountain bedecked with nymphs. Turn left at the sculpture and at the riverside path turn right. Continue ahead on the tarmac and through a wrought-iron gate to the sculpture garden. Turn right to leave via a metal gate. Turn right on Riverside and continue ahead, back to the pub.

The sculpture garden at York House

PLACES OF INTEREST NEARBY
Marble Hill House (admission charge) has a fine collection of paintings. It is open on Wednesday to Sunday: 10 am to 6 pm from April to October and 10 am to 4 pm from November to March. Telephone: 020 8892 5115. **Orleans House Art Gallery**, an 18th century octagonal pavilion in secluded woodland gardens, is open in the afternoons, Tuesday to Sunday and bank holidays; entry is free. Telephone: 020 8892 0221.

Hampton Wick
The White Hart

DIRECTIONS TO START: THE WHITE HART IS AT THE BEGINNING (NO 1) OF THE HIGH STREET IN HAMPTON WICK, NEXT TO THE ROUNDABOUT WHERE IT JOINS THE A308 AT KINGSTON BRIDGE. **STATIONS:** HAMPTON WICK OR KINGSTON. **PARKING:** AT THE PUB (PATRONS) OR THERE ARE CAR PARKS IN BUSHY PARK.

This walk takes you through Bushy Park, which was first enclosed for hunting by Henry VIII – the graceful statue of Diana, goddess of the hunt, is a reminder of its regal past. Its spacious vistas are still dotted with ponds and crossed by imposing avenues of trees, but the deer now roam in safety. You then continue along traditional Teddington High Street with plenty of opportunity to browse through antiques, books or bric-a-brac or take a break in a teashop. After reaching the Thames at Teddington Lock – the last of 45 locks before the river becomes tidal – the walk concludes with a stroll along the riverside path.

The White Hart

With its Grade II-listed façade, the White Hart looks like a hotel, but non-residents are welcome even if just popping in for a drink. The elegant bar has pewter ornaments, chandeliers and comfortable upholstered seating; outside, there are benches at the front of the building. This is a Fuller's House with ESB, London Pride and Jack Frost on handpump and a large selection of wines and bottled lagers. The menu is imaginative and varied. For example, for a light lunch you could choose baby octopus salad or Mediterranean terrine with tomato salad. More substantial fare includes lamb shank on mashed sweet potato with rosemary, and mushroom and ginger stroganoff with rice. Steaks, jacket potatoes and sandwiches are also served and there is a Sunday roast. Desserts include chocolate fudge cake, cheesecake, and fruit with yoghurt.

The bar is open all day; lunch is available from 12 noon every day, to 2.30 pm on Monday to Thursday, 5.30 pm on Friday and Saturday and 4 pm on Sunday. Evening meals are served on Monday to Saturday from 6 pm to 10 pm and on Sunday 6 pm to 9 pm. Telephone: 020 8977 1786.

The Walk

① Leave the pub and turn right onto Hampton Court Road. Take the first right onto Church Grove and continue ahead. Opposite the church of St John the Baptist, turn left through a narrow wrought-iron gate to enter Bushy Park. Continue ahead along the wide path lined with horse-

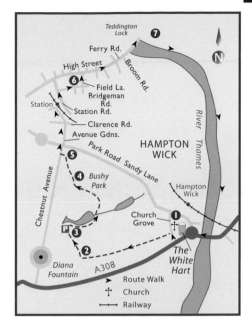

chestnut trees. Exit through the gate at the end and continue ahead on the tarmac, eventually passing toilets and a playground with sandpit on the left. Ahead is Chestnut Avenue and half right is the Diana Fountain.

② At the entrance to the sandpit turn right onto a narrow dirt path across the grass. Continue on this path as it veers slightly right towards a car park. Cross a tarmac path and continue ahead on a pebble path to the right of the car park.

③ Do not cross the bridge, but turn right to walk by Heron Pond. Continue ahead on this path as it curves left and crosses a bridge. After the bridge, when the perimeter path goes left to skirt the pond, continue straight ahead on a narrow ill-defined path through bracken. Continue to the T-junction and turn left onto the tarmacked Cobblers Walk.

Heron Pond

footbridge over the line onto Station Road. Turn left, then take the first right onto Bridgeman Road, cross the end of Cedar Road on the left and Blackmores Grove on the right and turn left onto Field Lane.

⑥ At the T-junction turn right onto Teddington High Street. Cross the end of Langham Road. Cross Kingston Road at the pedestrian lights, continue ahead and cross the end of Broom Road. Proceed ahead and cross the bridge over the Thames. Climb the steps to continue over the second section of the bridge, then take the steps down to the left.

⑦ Turn right along the tree-lined Thames path signposted 'Kingston Bridge 2 miles'. When you reach Lower Ham Road continue ahead along the pavement on the left hand side of road. At the end of the road regain the Thames Path and continue ahead. After going under the railway bridge, skirt around the Slug and Lettuce pub and continue to Kingston Bridge. Opposite the tunnel under the bridge, and facing the lower entrance to RB's Bar, turn left and ascend the steps to Kingston Bridge. Turn right, continue over the bridge and cross the road at the zebra crossing to return to the pub.

④ As you approach Chestnut Avenue, turn right just before the several rows of trees to the right of the avenue on a wide grass track, again through bracken. Follow the track as it curves left to divide the lines of trees. Ahead of you at the end of Chestnut Avenue is the exit gate onto Park Road. Turn left onto the tarmac and immediately right to exit the park by the pedestrian gate to the right of the road gate.

⑤ Turn right onto Park Road to cross it by the zebra crossing and continue ahead along Avenue Road. At the T-junction turn left and immediately right onto Victoria Road. Continue ahead, passing Teddington station on the right. Turn right immediately after the station building and cross the

PLACES OF INTEREST NEARBY
Hampton Court Palace (admission charge) is the largest and most impressive of the riverside royal palaces. Set in 60 acres of gardens (admission free), it is open from 9.30 am to 6 pm on Tuesday to Sunday and 10.30 am to 6 pm on Monday from mid-March to mid-October; the rest of the year it opens from 9.30 am to 4.30 pm Tuesday to Sunday and 10.30 am to 4.30 pm on Monday. Telephone: 020 8781 9500.

Ealing
The Grange Tavern

MAP: OS EXPLORER 173 (GR 183802)   **WALK 17**   **DISTANCE:** 2¼ MILES

DIRECTIONS TO START: BETWEEN THE A40 AND THE A4 THE NORTH CIRCULAR ROAD PASSES THE EAST SIDE OF EALING COMMON. WARWICK ROAD TURNS OFF THIS TO PASS THROUGH THE COMMON TO THE PUB ON THE WEST SIDE. **STATIONS:** EALING COMMON (DISTRICT, PICCADILLY), SOUTH EALING (PICCADILLY), EALING BROADWAY (CENTRAL, DISTRICT). **PARKING:** THE PUB HAS NO CAR PARK. MOST OF THE SURROUNDING STREETS ARE IN CONTROLLED ZONES. PAY CAR PARKS ARE PROVIDED BY EALING BROADWAY SHOPPING CENTRE.

This gentle, leisurely stroll takes in common land, a large pleasant park and a couple of leafy avenues in quiet parts of Ealing just off the North Circular Road and Ealing Broadway. Spencer Perceval, so far the only British Prime Minister to have been assassinated, in 1812, owned a house in Elm Grove, and near it, at the start of the walk, you pass the Spencer Perceval Memorial Church, built with a bequest from his daughter. Ealing Common comes next, part of which is left relatively untouched during summer to provide a habitat for wildlife. Walpole Park, which you visit next, used to be the grounds of Pitshanger Manor, now owned by the borough. All in all, a pleasant place to spend a summer's day – the walk is short, but you may want to linger on the common or in the park and just watch the world go by.

The Grange Tavern

A large Victorian brick corner building houses this family-friendly pub in a quiet side street off Ealing Common. It is beautifully situated – the main front bar overlooks the common, and is furnished with comfortable sofas. Food is served in a large conservatory bar, where the daily hot specials, traditional hearty pub favourites, are chalked up on a board. Salads and snacks, as well as desserts, are also available. The lunch dishes are served from 11 am (12 noon on Sunday) until 2.30 pm; some food is available all afternoon, and there is a separate table dining menu from 6 pm to 9.30 pm.

Courage Directors and Theakston ales are handpumped; some premium lagers are on draught. In warm weather the patio 'garden area', with a number of tables, is a pleasant leafy, shaded refuge. Barbecues occasionally take place here in the summer. A roots/folk music club meets here on most Wednesdays, and a comedy club uses the venue on alternate Sundays. Telephone: 020 8567 7617.

lines of chestnut trees marking Warwick Road. Cross the road and continue round the right hand side of the common. Cross another chestnut avenue and follow the trees to the left. Cross the road at the edge of the common and enter The Grove (just to the right of Grange Road).

Walpole Park

The Walk

① Leaving the pub, turn left towards the common, then right into Warwick Dene. Turn left at All Saints', the Spencer Perceval Memorial Church, into Elm Avenue, then walk onto the common. This part is left with long grass, which is mown at the end of summer, and has a horse track round the outside. Either take the tarmac path or walk across the grass to the

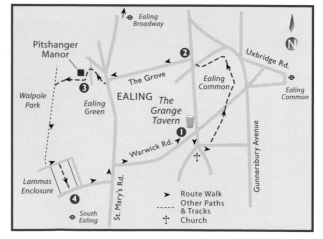

Ealing Common

② Walk down The Grove. Pass St Saviour's church/Clifton House; just a little further on you reach Ealing Green. Turn right, cross the High Street and walk towards the main gate into Walpole Park.

③ Walk to the left of Pitshanger Manor, passing the flower beds behind it, and turn left onto a path through the trees. At a children's playground, turn half left, pass an aviary on the left, and walk down the avenue. Many of the oaks lining the path are dedicated to former mayors of Ealing. Leave the park through the gate onto Lammas Park Gardens. Cross over, turn left, then turn right through the break in the hedge into the piece of land called Lammas Enclosure. Walk past the tennis courts and then the areas left wild for plants and insects.

④ Exit onto Beaconsfield Road, turn left, and turn left again at St Mary's Road, which has a broad tree-lined central reservation. Just before the Thames Valley University building, turn right into Warwick Road, and follow it back to the pub.

PLACES OF INTEREST NEARBY

Pitshanger Manor, which you pass on the walk, is open free as a local museum. The building is of architectural interest, as it was largely rebuilt in the early 19th century by John Soane, who also created the well-known idiosyncratic house in Lincoln's Inn Fields. Soane sold the estate in 1810, and the house has been splendidly refurbished for its role as a museum.

Kingsbury
The Prince of Wales

| MAP: OS EXPLORER 173 (GR 192888) | WALK 18 | DISTANCE: 3 MILES |

DIRECTIONS TO START: THE PUB IS AT THE JUNCTION OF KINGSBURY ROAD, HONEYPOT LANE, KENTON ROAD AND FRYENT WAY AT KINGSBURY, NW9. **STATION:** KINGSBURY (JUBILEE LINE). **PARKING:** THERE IS A SMALL CAR PARK AT THE PUB. ASK IF YOU MAY LEAVE YOUR CAR THERE WHILE YOU WALK. THERE IS A CAR PARK AT FRYENT COUNTRY PARK, ON THE WEST SIDE OF FRYENT WAY.

The mature woodland and hay meadows of Fryent Country Park represent one of the best surviving areas of traditional countryside in Middlesex. After passing through meadowland, the walk climbs steadily through woodland up to Barn Hill. Human history breaks into this very natural landscape at one point, in the form of the graceful Lombardy poplars lining the path: these were planted in 1935 to commemorate George V's Silver Jubilee. The expansive view from the summit of Barn Hill Open Space includes Wembley Stadium at the time of writing. You return to the pub through more meadows.

The Prince of Wales

This large, typical city pub has a lounge bar at one side where meals are served and a public bar at the other side with a pool table and other games. It's a Six Continents house with Tetley Bitter on handpump. Steak dishes are the pub's speciality, served on wooden skillets and delivered to the tables still sizzling. A choice of two roasts is available on Sunday.

Opening times are the standard pub hours, with food served from 12 noon to 3 pm and 6 pm to 8 pm on Monday to Friday and 12 noon to 5 pm on Saturday and Sunday. Children are welcome if they are eating. Dogs are not allowed. There is no garden, but on sunny days the benches at the front are a popular spot. Telephone: 020 8238 9020.

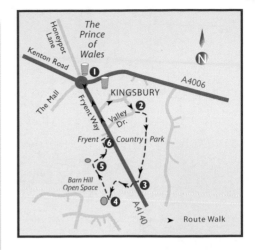

The Walk

① Exit the pub, turn left and walk along Kingsbury Road. Cross at the zebra crossing and turn right to walk towards the roundabout. Turn left onto Fryent Way and continue ahead, passing the entrance to Gore Court. Cross the bridge over the railway line and turn left onto Wyndale Avenue. At the T-junction with Valley Drive turn right and continue ahead.

② Where the road curves right, turn left to follow a footpath sign to Slough Lane. Pass between a fence and a wooden gate and then two concrete posts to enter Fryent Country Park. Veer slightly right on the path which goes gradually uphill across the middle of an expanse of grassland. Eventually this path goes gradually downhill and through a gap in a hedge.

After going through the gap veer slightly right to go ahead, keeping a line of shrubbery to your left. Go through another hedge gap and continue ahead on a path across a wide flat meadow. Go through a gap in a row of saplings and then through a gap in shrubbery and trees. Then go straight ahead on a slightly uphill path. At the top of this incline there is a two-armed 'circular walks' signpost. Continue ahead, following this signpost to reach Fryent Way.

③ Cross the road with care and veer slightly left to take a path veering slightly right into the woodland of Barn Hill. Continue ahead and, after passing between two wooden benches, turn left onto a path. Pass a three-armed signpost and continue on this path, lined with Lombardy poplars. At the T-junction veer right and continue to a pond with waterfowl. Turn left and follow the path to the white triangulation point marking the summit of Barn Hill Open Space. From the white triangulation point retrace your steps back to the right side of the pond.

Fryent Country Park

④ Stand facing the pond with your back to the poplar-lined path. Turn right and then take the first right by a black wooden post onto a wide downhill path. Keep on this path until you reach open grassland. Then continue ahead with the grassland on your right and trees to your left.

⑤ At the end of this grassland, turn right to pass a pond on your left. Continue ahead, keeping close to shrubbery on the left. Pass the end of a ditch on your right and at the next crosspaths, with Fryent Way visible ahead, turn left to go through a gap in the hedge. Continue ahead veering slightly right to keep near the line of hedge and trees on the right. Look out for a gap in this line about two thirds of the way along, and turn right to go through it. Then turn left so the trees are on your left and

Fryent Way is on the right. Keep going through another gap in trees. Now, ahead is a small piece of grassland and beyond it a row of houses. Turn right and continue ahead to emerge onto Fryent Way near a footpath sign.

⑥ Turn left onto Fryent Way and continue to the pub.

PLACES OF INTEREST NEARBY

The huge Shri Swaminarayan Mandir Temple was the first traditional Hindu temple to be built in Europe. This beautiful, striking building is open daily from 9.30 am to 6 pm. Admission is free, except to the interesting *Understanding Hinduism* exhibition. The temple is on Brentfield Road, NW10, just south of the A406 North Circular Road. Telephone: 020 8965 2651.

Gunnersbury Triangle
The Bollo House

| **MAP:** OS EXPLORER 161 (GR 202788) | **WALK 19** | **DISTANCE:** 2¼ MILES |

DIRECTIONS TO START: THE PUB IS AT 13–15 BOLLO LANE (CORNER OF MONTGOMERY ROAD), WHICH RUNS FROM THE A4000 GUNNERSBURY LANE TO ACTON LANE, JUST OFF THE A315 CHISWICK HIGH ROAD. **STATIONS:** CHISWICK PARK (DISTRICT), GUNNERSBURY (DISTRICT, SUBURBAN RAIL), ACTON TOWN (SUBURBAN RAIL). **PARKING:** THE PUB HAS NO CAR PARK. TRY ON-STREET, OR THERE IS A CAR PARK NEAR CHISWICK COMMON.

Gunnersbury Triangle is a gem of a Local Nature Reserve, managed by the London Wildlife Trust. Cut off from its surroundings by a triangle of railway lines, it has had a history of mixed use, and was threatened by redevelopment. In a pioneering case, it was finally preserved for conservation in the 1980s. This small area packs in woods, open grassland and a pond, and there's always something to see. Leaflets are available from Trust staff describing the features.

Afterwards, you see the pleasant expanse of Turnham Green, and pass Voysey House, a local building of interest originally belonging to a wallpaper manufacturer. Chiswick Common comes next, and then the Tabard Inn and St Michael's church, a group of buildings designed by the celebrated architect Norman Shaw. They face Acton Green Common where Prince Rupert's Royalist army defeated Lord Essex's parliamentary forces in the Battle of Brentford in 1642, during the Civil War.

The Bollo House

This established corner pub has been attractively refurbished into a 'gastro-pub', where food is taken seriously. A daily changing menu has a range of imaginative, mouthwatering dishes, naturally at the higher end of pub prices, with the lunch dish of the day being good value. Fish and seafood are usually well represented, and the desserts are very tempting. Snacks and delicious fresh sandwiches are also available at lunchtime. Tables are set out in the large open-plan interior, and on the pavement outside, enclosed by a wall of flower boxes. Bollo Lane is fairly quiet, and this is very pleasant in summer. Greene King ales and continental lagers are available, and there is an extensive wine list. Lunch and dinner are served and the pub is open all day from 12 noon. Telephone: 020 8994 6037.

The Walk

① Leaving the pub, turn left down Bollo Lane towards Chiswick Park. Go under the railway line and turn right into the nature reserve through the kissing gate, which is never locked. Information is available from the cabin on the left when it is staffed. Otherwise follow the path overlooking the District Line down to a main path. Numbered points guide your way through the reserve. Turn left at '2' and left again onto a minor path at '3' to walk through ferns and ivy-covered trees. Turn left again at '6' and follow the path round to the open glade. Retrace your steps to '7', then fork left. Climb steps to gain a view of the tree canopy, then follow steps down to the pond. The railway line to the left is the North London suburban line. Follow the path round to the right at the open grassland at '13' and walk back along the ballast of an abandoned railway track to the entrance. Turn right and right again onto Acton Lane over the bridge.

② Cross Chiswick High Road, turn left and cross onto Turnham Green. Walk across it on the diagonal path towards the church. The Town Hall is on the right. Cross the central Town Hall Avenue and walk past the church and across the green towards the war memorial. Notice the white brick building on the right with square chimneys and scalloped walls, Voysey House. Leave the green via the gate, cross Heathfield Terrace, turn right and turn left into Barley Mow Passage to get a closer look at Voysey House. Turn left down the passage between Voysey House and the pub and cross the High Road. Turn right, pass the Catholic church opposite and turn left down Fishers Lane.

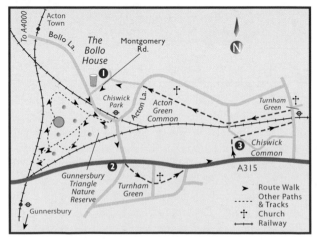

The Nature Reserve is cut off by railway tracks

③ Turn half right at Chiswick Common. Walk towards Turnham Green station; turn left here under the bridge. Opposite, at the end of Bath Road, note the Tabard Inn and church of St Michael and All Angels. Turn left onto Acton Green Common. Walk across the common, crossing Fishers Lane, which bisects it. At the end, cross Acton Lane into Cunnington Street, then turn left into Montgomery Road to return to the pub.

PLACES OF INTEREST NEARBY

If your botanical interests have been stimulated, **Kew Gardens** are close at hand over the river. These internationally renowned botanical gardens are just a short ride from Acton Town or Turnham Green. There is a good website to help you plan a visit at www.rbgkew.org.uk, or telephone 020 8332 5000 for details of opening times and admission charges.

Chiswick
The Mawson Arms

MAP: OS EXPLORER 161 (GR 216780) — **WALK 20** — **DISTANCE:** 3½ MILES

DIRECTIONS TO START: THE PUB IS ON MAWSON LANE ON THE CORNER OF CHISWICK LANE SOUTH. TURN SOUTH FROM THE GREAT WEST ROAD (A4) JUST BEFORE THE HOGARTH ROUNDABOUT. **STATIONS:** CHISWICK STATION IS NEAR POINTS 7 AND 8; **UNDERGROUND:** TURNHAM GREEN (DISTRICT LINE). BUSES: E3, H91, 27, 237, 267, 391 TO CHISWICK HIGH STREET. BUS 190 STOPS VERY NEAR THE PUB IN CHISWICK LANE. **PARKING:** THERE IS NO PUB CAR PARK; TRY ON-STREET ON EITHER SIDE OF THE A4.

Setting out from a building where the poet Alexander Pope once lived, this is a pleasant stroll through an 18th century landscape. First you walk down tree-lined streets of fine old Georgian houses, and on to a timeless path beside the river. Then take a walk through the grounds of Chiswick House, admiring the classical temple and obelisk. The route back passes the home of William Hogarth, where a large collection of the artist's work is well worth a look.

The Mawson Arms

This pub though generally known as the Mawson Arms, also boasts a pub sign proclaiming it to be the Fox and Hounds. Many stories circulate as to why it has two names and the one told to us is that sometime in the 19th century two Fuller's brothers had a heated argument after which they refused to speak to each other. One of them had a wall built to separate the bar in two and renamed his side the Mawson Arms. The wall has long gone so who knows?

The pub is attached to the Fuller, Smith & Turner's Griffin Brewery – London's oldest, on this site since the mid-1660s – so, naturally, a full range of Fuller's beers is available on handpump, including one of their delightful seasonal ales. The pub's large, plain bar is quite atmospheric and comfortable with bare boards, stripped wood benches and chairs, and black-and-white photographs of the brewery in times gone by.

The menu, chalked on a board, includes dishes such as lasagne, ham and eggs, Cajun chicken, beef and ale pie and veggie burger as well as sandwiches, ploughman's lunches and filled jacket potatoes. Children may eat inside. Dogs are allowed in after 3 pm. Note the restricted opening hours: from 11 am to 8 pm on weekdays, closed at weekends. Food is served from 12 noon to 3 pm. Telephone: 020 8994 2936. When the pub is closed, try the George and Devonshire instead. Telephone: 0208 994 1859.

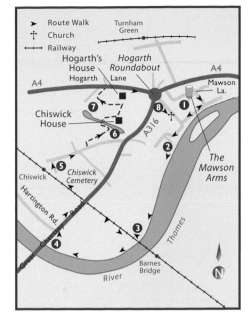

The Walk

① From the pub turn right and right again onto Chiswick Lane South, passing the Brewery Store. At the river, flowing past Chiswick Eyot, turn right along Chiswick Mall with Georgian houses on the right.

② When Chiswick Mall curves right, turn left through the metal gate onto a path, turning right along Thames Crescent and then a tree-lined tarmac path following the river. Pass the Riverside Recreation Ground. At the bandstand continue ahead on the riverside path. After passing Emmanuel School Boat House on the right, descend four steps to continue along the tarmac path.

③ Just before the steps at Barnes Bridge, turn right onto a tarmac path between wire fences. Continue on a wide pavement following the embankment to Esporta

Riverside Club on the right. Turn left opposite the sports centre under the bridge (following a Thames Path sign). Follow the road to the left with care – there is no footpath. Opposite Chiswick RFC on the right, pass Duke's Hollow Nature Reserve, then continue as the road snakes to the river. Here, turn right onto the narrow dirt path between river and road. Pass the car park on the right. Walk around the UMDS Boat Club building on the left, then veer left towards the river, going through the boatyard.

④ Climb the steps and turn right onto Great Chertsey Road. Go to the traffic lights at the end of Hartington Road. Turn left, cross, then turn right and continue along Great Chertsey Road as far as the railway bridge. Cross and turn left down the steps. Turn left and immediately right along a tarmac track between the railway embankment and the cemetery. Follow this path to Burlington Lane, just right of Chiswick station.

⑤ Turn right and go along Burlington Lane, crossing Staveley Road, following a sign for Chiswick House and grounds and Hogarth's House. Take the first left through the iron gates into Chiswick House grounds. Walk ahead to the obelisk, then veer right. You come to a lake, ahead and to the left, and beyond it Chiswick House.

⑥ Turn left to walk along the left side of the lake. Pass a classical temple on the far side of the lake. Turn right across a bridge. At the far side, veer right and walk along a wide dirt track between boxed hedges, with the lake across the grass on your right. Pass the front of the temple on your right behind a circular pond with an obelisk. Continue along the wide avenue to the back of Chiswick House. If you are visiting the house, walk round to the front. Otherwise, turn left and go straight on through the gate in the archway. At the crosspaths veer right and at the next crosspaths turn right, passing the café over to the right. Turn left with the path and continue ahead.

⑦ At the conservatory on the left, turn right on the tarmac and then left at the T-junction to walk towards the exit onto the A4. Just before the gates turn right on a tarmac track signposted to Hogarth's House. Turn left with the path and leave it through a narrow iron gate onto Hogarth Lane (A4). Turn right, passing Hogarth's House on the right. Go under the subway and follow the signpost to Church Street, Burlington Lane South and Chertsey Road.

⑧ Exit the subway, pass the George and Devonshire pub on the right, turn right and go along Church Street, passing Chiswick parish church on the right. At the T-junction turn left onto Chiswick Mall, then left onto Chiswick Lane South and return to the pub.

PLACES OF INTEREST NEARBY
Hogarth's House (free) is open from 1 pm to 5 pm on Tuesday to Sunday. Telephone: 020 8994 6757. **Griffin Brewery tours** are held on Monday, Wednesday, Thursday and Friday at 11 am, 12 noon, 1 pm and 2 pm. Book in advance. Telephone: 020 8996 2063.

Welsh Harp
The Harp

| MAP: OS EXPLORER 173 (GR 222878) | **WALK 21** | DISTANCE: 3 MILES |

DIRECTIONS TO START: THE PUB IS ON THE CORNER OF THE BROADWAY (A5)
AND COOL OAK LANE IN WEST HENDON, JUST NORTH OF STAPLES CORNER.
STATION: HENDON. **PARKING:** IN THE PUB CAR PARK, OR USE THE FREE CAR PARK ON
PERRYFIELD WAY, JUST WEST OF THE BROADWAY.

This walk takes you through the woodlands and meadows fringing the Brent Reservoir (better known as the Welsh Harp) – an excellent habitat for waterfowl. The reservoir was established in 1835 as a feeder for the Grand Union Canal, rather than for drinking water, so relatively close access is possible and it is a popular spot for sailing. Part of the site, 69 acres, was designated a Site of Special Scientific Interest in 1950. Up to 140 species of birds have been recorded here.

The Harp

This typical city pub has a large open plan interior and traditional décor with wood-panelled walls and comfortable upholstered seating. There is a good range of draught and bottled lagers and wines and Guinness Extra Gold on handpump. It's a friendly family-run pub serving home-made dishes with well-prepared fresh vegetables. As well as daily specials, which always include a vegetarian dish, lamb and beef roast with Yorkshire pudding and an all-day breakfast are served every day. Sandwiches and filled jacket potatoes are also available. Children are welcome if they are eating (indoors only as there is no garden). The Harp is open during standard pub hours and food is served daily from 12 noon to 7 pm. Telephone: 020 8202 6793.

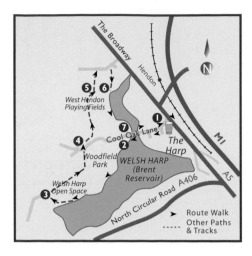

The Walk

① Leaving the pub, turn left and then left again onto Cool Oak Lane and continue ahead. Cross over the end of Esmar Crescent and then Woolmead Avenue. Pass the Welsh Harp Youth Sailing base and then, with great care as there is no footpath, cross the bridge.

② Once over the bridge veer left onto a wide earth path, passing a Welsh Harp Reservoir information board on the right, and a little further along on the left an observation platform overlooking the reservoir. Continue ahead, going slightly uphill and keeping on the main path, ignoring all turn-offs, and eventually passing a playing field on the right. When the earth track becomes tarmac continue ahead and soon the spire of St Andrew's church is visible ahead and there are good views of the reservoir to the left.

③ Just beyond a metal car barrier, and before a tarmac road, turn sharp right onto a narrow tarmac path. Continue ahead on this winding path which eventually passes a playing field on the right and Woodfield School on the left. Cross the small car park and walk to Wood Lane along the approach road to the school.

④ Cross over Wood Lane, turn right and continue ahead on the pavement. Cross the end of Kinloch Drive and continue ahead. Where the pavement ends veer left to walk in the same direction along a narrow tarmac path parallel with, and to the left of, the road. Just before the end of the tarmac path veer left on a narrow grassy path. Continue ahead, passing a playing field and the back of a goal mouth on your right. At the end of the playing field keep on this path which is now wider and downhill. When it levels out continue ahead, passing another playing field on the right. After

Brent Reservoir

passing a large oak tree on the left go straight ahead towards the houses; there is another playing field on the right. Keep near the shrubbery on the left.

⑤ Just beyond the playing field, and after passing a line of shrubbery and trees on your right, turn right to walk to the left of the line of trees and shrubbery. At the end of the field turn left with the path and shrubbery and walk towards the houses. At the wooden fence turn right to pass the end of trees and shrubbery on the right. Continue ahead and soon veer slightly right to reach a children's playground ahead. At the T-junction with the wide metal track, and to the right of the children's playground, turn right and go ahead.

⑥ Shortly before a T-junction and a bench on the right, and opposite a bowling green, veer left to walk across the grass to the left of a line of trees and shrubbery. Keep going when very soon there is shrubbery on both sides. Ignore a turning left and keep going on the main path. At the T-junction of paths veer left and continue ahead. Ignore a turn to the right and continue ahead. You may catch a glimpse of the reservoir on the left. Ignore another right turn and continue ahead. Eventually the path becomes a brown dirt track. Pass two benches, one on each side of the track, and continue ahead to Cool Oak Lane.

⑦ Turn left, cross the bridge and continue ahead, back to the pub.

PLACES OF INTEREST NEARBY

The excellent **Royal Air Force Museum** charts the history of aviation and the RAF. Displays of combat aircraft include the Spitfire, Typhoon and Lancaster. A 'sound and light' show tells the story of the Battle of Britain. The museum is at Grahame Park Way, NW9 (set off north up the A5). Opening times are 10 am to 6 pm daily. Telephone: 020 8205 2266.

Barnet Gate
The Gate

MAP: OS EXPLORER 173 (GR 217951) **WALK 22** **DISTANCE:** 1½ OR 3 MILES

DIRECTIONS TO START: THE PUB IS AT THE JUNCTION OF THE A411 BARNET ROAD WITH HENDON WOOD LANE (B552). THE A411 MEETS THE A1 AT STIRLING CORNER. **STATION:** HIGH BARNET (NORTHERN), THEN WALK OR TAKE BUS 107, WESTWARDS ALONG THE A411. **PARKING:** PLEASE DON'T LEAVE CARS IN THE PUB CAR PARK WHEN YOU'RE WALKING. USE THE CAR PARK FOR MOAT MOUNT NATURE RESERVE, OFF THE SOUTHBOUND A1 (NEAR POINT 5).

This is a very rural area of Barnet. The walk starts off through woods, and beside fields shaded by oaks and chestnuts, near Barnet Gate Wood, a local nature reserve, which can be visited as a diversion. The walk continues through Moat Mount Open Space, before entering Moat Mount Local Nature Reserve, which is situated in the former grounds of Moat Mount House. This includes wild habitat, undergrowth, streams, some native trees and exotics, like a giant sequoia, planted 200 years ago, and the Leg of Mutton Pond. It is a haven for all types of wildlife. A short cut is possible, omitting the nature reserve, by going straight from the start of point 3 to point 6.

The Gate

There has been a pub here for some while, previously under the name of the Bell. It has recently been refurbished with the emphasis on supplying food, which is cooked to order from standard and vegetarian menus. Both menus have a range of very generously sized starters and main courses, with specials chalked up on separate boards. The food is good, with some imaginative choices. There are plenty of tables, distributed among a front flagstoned bar, a rear bar with floorboards, a carpeted extension (so you can choose your floor covering) and a no-smoking conservatory. Children can dine with their parents, and there is also a large garden. Desserts and coffee make up a full meal. Food is served from 12 noon to 10 pm (9 pm on Sundays). Three ales are available on handpump: Young's, Adnams and Greene King Abbot. There is also a choice of wines. Telephone: 020 8449 7292.

The Walk

NB: Be prepared for some muddy patches in the nature reserve.

① Leave the pub, turn left and left again down Hendon Wood Lane on the right hand side. Just before Tree Lodge (three or four houses down), turn right onto the public footpath to 'Barnet Gate Wood, Mill Hill & Moat Mount Open Space'. Go through a kissing gate, then at the end of the path turn left downhill; do not enter the field. Go through the wood.

② At a T-junction turn right onto a path waymarked 'Dollis Valley Greenwalk' (DVG), 'London Loop' and 'Barnet Countryside Leisure Walks 8'. Turn left at the start of the next field and follow the arrows down a fenced path. Go through a kissing gate and follow the path round to the half right. Go through another solo kissing gate.

③ Go through a pair of kissing gates either side of a farm track, keeping to the DVG, fenced off from the field. Shortly after, cross another farm track with kissing gates either side, still following the London Loop and DVG arrows along the fenced path.

④ Enter Moat Mount Local Nature Reserve. Turn left following the arrow. Follow the path down by a stream through woods, pass the outdoor centre on the opposite side of the stream, and then go up a set of wooden steps. Turn left to go up an avenue of hornbeams on a tarmac path that leads to the Leg of Mutton Pond.

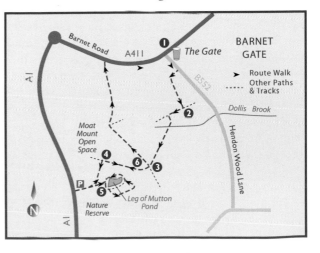

Moat Mount Open Space

⑤ Turn right to walk round the pond. At the end of a concrete embankment, continue straight on past the giant sequoia tree and then uphill (following a blue arrow), passing a (signposted) giant Wellingtonia on the right. Further up, turn half left towards a wooden fence – follow this past where it becomes a wire fence, then turn left onto a clear but narrow path downhill, passing rhododendrons and fir trees. Come back to the Leg of Mutton Pond, continue with it on the left, and turn right onto the first tarmac path, just past a bench. Now retrace your steps to the start of point 3, immediately after having returned through the second set of kissing gates.

⑥ Now go through the kissing gate leading onto a path diagonally across the field. At the hedge go through the kissing gate. Follow the public footpath sign to Stirling Common. Walk across the field to the far right corner, then turn right onto an uphill path with a fence and hedge on the left (not the path heading towards Barnet Gate Wood). Continue along through a kissing gate over a sleeper bridge, heading for the road. Go through the last kissing gate onto the road and cross it to the footpath. Turn right, and walk back to the Gate.

PLACES OF INTEREST NEARBY
The **Tree Trail** in Moat Mount Local Nature Reserve takes advantage of the mix of exotic and native species planted in the former private park. Trees of interest have explanatory signs, and it takes about 45 minutes to walk round them all. Leaflets are available in Barnet libraries.

Kensal Green
Paradise by Way of Kensal Green

MAP: OS EXPLORER 173 (GR 238826) · **WALK 23** · **DISTANCE:** 2½ MILES

DIRECTIONS TO START: THE PUB IS AT 19 KILBURN LANE, JUST OFF THE A404 HARROW ROAD WHERE IT MEETS LADBROKE GROVE. **STATIONS:** KENSAL GREEN (BAKERLOO AND SUBURBAN RAIL); WILLESDEN JUNCTION (BAKERLOO AND SUBURBAN RAIL). **PARKING:** THE PUB HAS NO CAR PARK. TRY ON-STREET, OR COME BY PUBLIC TRANSPORT.

'The Library' and main bar of the Paradise

Kensal Green Cemetery is one of London's magnificent graveyards, pre-Victorian as it was founded in 1830. It became fashionable when chosen by two of George III's children – Augustus Frederick, who wanted to be buried next to a disapproved-of wife, and Sophie who had had an illegitimate child by an equerry.

You start on the towpath of the Grand Union Canal. This is a wonderful slice of green in an urban area, especially the Canal Gasworks Conservation Area, a thin strip of land between the railway and canal. You return via two cemeteries, first the neatly laid-out St Mary's Roman Catholic Cemetery. Kensal Green Cemetery has many overgrown parts, which are a real wildlife resource, and picturesque overgrown monuments. Maps showing notable burial sites may be bought from the office at the entrance.

Paradise by Way of Kensal Green

Outside it may be Kensal Green, but inside it's Paradise. A six-foot angel statue watches over the large front bar, and there's a side room, the library, and a separate restaurant at the back, with a small courtyard. G.K. Chesterton's poem *The Rolling English Road*, from which the pub name is taken, adorns the front of the bar.

Although this building is Victorian, there has been a pub on the site since 1645. Shepherd Neame Spitfire ale is kept in the original cellars. Hoegaarden is also available, and there is a good selection of wines. The food, lunch and a separate evening menu, is delicious – definitely upmarket 'gastropub' quality. Arrive hungry, as there are tempting starters, such as Parma ham with balsamic roasted figs or home-made soup, substantial main courses, such as a gourmet sausage and mash, roast duck breast or monkfish, and desirable desserts such as sticky toffee pudding made with dates, or Kahlua crème brûlée. No need to rush, as the restaurant serves lunch from 12 noon to 4 pm. You can always do the walk tomorrow. This pub is – heavenly. Telephone: 020 8969 0098.

The Walk

① From the pub, turn right, cross Harrow Road at the lights and go straight on into Ladbroke Grove. Pass the Dissenters' Chapel, cross over the canal then turn right onto the paved towpath. Pass the Canalside Activity Centre, and cross the footbridge over a canal basin. Pass the supermarket and cross another footbridge over a basin. Pass the gas holders on the left, then turn left onto a gravel path leading through the Canal Gasworks Conservation Area back to the towpath. Go under the road bridge, and leave the towpath to go up onto Scrubs Lane.

② Take in the painted mural on the bridge, cross over to the right hand side, and turn left. Continue along Scrubs Lane until the road rises before a bridge. Turn right through the gate into St Mary's Roman Catholic Cemetery.

③ Follow first a path, which becomes a road across the north end of the cemetery, passing several mausoleums. Just past the chapel, pass a number of military graves on the right. A little further to the right is a monument to Belgian soldiers of the Second World War. Continue parallel to the railway, passing the lodge to the exit, and turn right onto the drive from Harrow Road leading into the main cemetery.

④ Walk down from the entrance and turn half left onto the broad curve of Oxford Avenue. Turn left onto the main West Centre Avenue. This sweeps to the left, passing, on the left, the mausoleum of the Duke of Cambridge, a grandson of George III, then on the right the grave of the tightrope walker Blondin. Carry on to the

---

PLACES OF INTEREST NEARBY

There is a **guided tour of the cemetery** by Friends of Kensal Green Cemetery every Sunday at 2 pm starting at the Anglican Chapel (fee). **The Catacombs** below the chapel (which are otherwise locked) are included on the first Sunday of every month.

Kensal Green Cemetery

Anglican Chapel, walk past it and then down the steps onto the main Centre Avenue. Walk between the two imposing royal tombs and keep along this path.

⑤ After crossing Junction Avenue, you pass many of the grandest Victorian memorials. Watch out for the extravagant Egyptian-style mausoleum of Ducrow, soon on your right, then later, on the same side, Casement's monument with four turban-wearing supporters, like Greek caryatids. Follow Centre Avenue past the junction with North Avenue, then round to the main

gateway on the left. Outside, turn right onto Harrow Road, then left into Kilburn Lane to return to the pub.

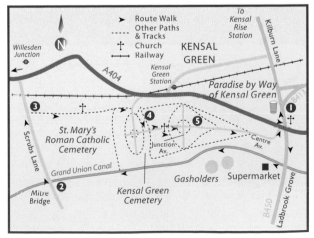

Fulham
The White Horse

MAP: OS EXPLORER 161 (GR 251766)   WALK 24   DISTANCE: 4 MILES

DIRECTIONS TO START: THE PUB IS AT 1–3 PARSONS GREEN, JUST OFF THE A308, NEW KINGS ROAD, BETWEEN PUTNEY BRIDGE AND WANDSWORTH BRIDGE. **STATION:** PARSONS GREEN (DISTRICT). **PARKING:** THE PUB HAS NO CAR PARK; THERE IS METER PARKING IN THE AREA.

Some surviving urban green areas and a slice of the riverside make up this walk. From Parsons Green, named for a parsonage, and formerly the site of pleasure fairs and then of cricket matches, you continue to Eel Brook Common and on to near the site of Cremorne Gardens. The site of these pleasure gardens disappeared in 1905 under Lots Road power station. The power station, no longer needed by the Underground, waits to be converted into luxury flats.

Redevelopment has made the riverside accessible, giving fine views of the river, its plentiful birdlife, and the busy heliport. Although redevelopment is far from complete at the time of writing, in the future the Thames Path will run from Chelsea Harbour to the supermarket car park in point 3. The walk ends near the private Hurlingham Club, founded for shooting pigeons, and once the home of polo, but the polo ground is now in a public park. Check fixtures for Chelsea and Fulham in the football season – their grounds are near the walk.

The White Horse

There has been a coaching inn on Parsons Green since the 17th century – this building overlooking the green is Victorian and has been attractively refurbished. There is one huge front bar, with lots of tables and chairs, and soft sofas, and plenty of light from the tall windows, and a separate restaurant. In fine weather the patio area in front feels like a continuation of the green.

There is a great choice of specialist bottled lagers here, and a wine list. Ales from five sets of handpumps include Adnams Broadside, Bass Bitter, Rooster's Yankee and Highgate & Walsall Dark Mild. Some beers are also obtained from the Freedom Brewery across the road. Food here is of a gourmet standard, from doorstep-size fresh sandwiches to hot meals. They're good on fish, game and duck, with satisfying large portions, but do leave room for a dessert. Meals and snacks are served all day until 10 pm at weekends. On weekdays the full menu is available from 11.30 am to 3 pm and from 6 pm to 10 pm; sandwiches and snacks can be ordered from 3 pm to 6 pm. Telephone: 020 7736 2115.

The Walk

① From the pub, cross onto Parsons Green and walk across it, turn left at the end and walk down New King's Road. Cross Molesford Road, take the left fork, and continue along Crondace Road, beside the tree-ringed lawns. At the end of Crondace Road, take the path to the half-left across Eel Brook Common, which is surrounded by plane trees. At the end of the grass, go up to street level and continue along Musgrave Crescent to the end, then turn right into Moore Park Road. Cross Harwood Road, with Fulham Town Hall on the left. Continue down Moore Park Road, crossing Waterford Road and Britannia Road.

② Just before Fulham Broadway, turn right onto Holmead Road. Turn left into Kings Road, then right into Lots Road, by the store with the clocktower. Turn left into Westfield Park, a small park made out of pedestrianised streets. Follow the main path through to the right and then left, and leave by the gate on Upcerne Road facing the power station. Walk down past the art school and turn right at the Lots Road power station. Turn left into Chelsea Harbour following the Thames Path sign. Cross the bridge, walk into Chelsea Harbour Estate through the gateway, turn left following the sign along Chelsea Harbour Drive. The road turns to the right to give you a view of the river, including Battersea and Albert bridges and the London Eye. Turn right and walk down to the river between the chestnuts, and turn right onto the Thames Path. Note the 1777 riverside church opposite, St Mary's Battersea, the only Grade I listed building in Wandsworth.

> ### PLACES OF INTEREST NEARBY
> **Brompton Cemetery**, founded in 1837, now comes under the Royal Parks Agency. Notable people buried here include Emmeline Pankhurst and Dr John Snow, who identified the cause of cholera. The entrances are on Fulham Road (A304) and Old Brompton Road (A3218); opening hours are basically daylight, until 8 pm in summer, 6 pm in spring and autumn and 4 pm in winter. Telephone: 020 7352 1201.

The church of St Mary's Battersea seen across the river

regain the river. Pass a supermarket built on the site of Fulham power station coaling yard – this is marked by crane rails and bollards along the path. Just past the building, turn right through the car park, and turn left at the road.

④ Cross Wandsworth Bridge Road and continue down Carnwath Road to its end and turn right into Broomhouse Lane, passing the private Hurlingham Sports Club grounds, then Hurlingham Park. Enter the park through the gateway and walk across it to Hurlingham Road. Turn right out of the gateway onto the road and turn left at Linver Road. Turn right at New King's Road and then left at Parsons Green to return to the pub.

③ Cross the entrance to the marina on the Dutch-style bascule bridge. At the rail bridge, turn right following the Thames Path sign, and at the road junction turn left under the railway, and follow Townmead Road past the redevelopment extending the riverside path. Turn left at Watermeadow Lane, and left again at William Morris Way. Turn right following the Thames Path sign to

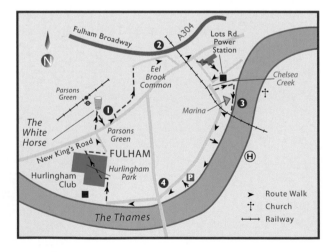

Little Venice
The Warwick Castle

MAP: OS EXPLORER 173 (GR 261819) | **WALK 25** | DISTANCE: 1¾ MILES

DIRECTIONS TO START: WARWICK PLACE IS OFF WARWICK AVENUE BY THE CANAL,
NOT FAR FROM WHERE THE A5, EDGWARE ROAD, MEETS THE A40.
STATION: WARWICK AVENUE (BAKERLOO). **PARKING:** THE PUB HAS NO CAR PARK;
ON-STREET 'IS DREADFUL' SAY BAR STAFF. COME BY PUBLIC TRANSPORT.

Little Venice is one of the most attractive parts of the canal system in London. It is formed by the junction of the Regent's Canal, the Grand Union Canal and Paddington Basin. A small island here adds to the scenery produced by trees, waterfowl and the backdrop of the canalside Rembrandt Gardens. In addition there is the life of the canal: it's a starting point for boat trips, canal boats are constantly gliding past, there's a Floating Art Gallery, floating restaurants and highly prized long-term moorings for houseboats – some with elaborate canalside gardens and even a rockery. This relaxing stroll also gives a glimpse of Paddington Basin, currently in the throes of redevelopment, and of Paddington Green, before returning via the end of the Maida Vale canal tunnel and the towpath. Much of the route is overlooked by fine villas.

The Warwick Castle

This large, friendly pub is on a quiet side street just off the canal. In summer there are tables outside on the pavement, and inside there is a large main bar. Bass and Fuller's London Pride are on hand-pumps, and Hoegaarden, Staropramen and Grolsch are also on tap. 'Only the best here', said a grinning barman, referring to the genuine Czech Budvar Budweiser.

The same principle seems to apply to the food; even the sandwiches feature corn-fed chicken, Berkshire ham or prize-winning sausages. Wild mushrooms figure prominently in a number of starters and main courses. Do try the house speciality of sausages and chive-flavoured mash with red onion gravy. Greek salad and pasta with a sauce of wild mushroom, courgette, pine nut and baby spinach are examples of vegetarian dishes available. Children may eat in the large back room, but not the main bar.

Food is only served at lunchtimes – until 2 pm on weekdays or 2.30 pm at weekends. The pub's opening times are: Monday to Thursday 12 noon to 2.30 pm and 5 pm to 11 pm, Friday and Saturday 12 noon to 11 pm, Sunday 12 noon to 10.30 pm. Telephone: 020 7432 1331.

The Walk

① Turn right from the pub, walk to the end of Warwick Place, and turn right again onto Blomfield Road. Pass the end of Clifton Villas, with a view of the church, then cross the canal via the footbridge at the end of Formosa Street.

② Turn left onto Delamere Terrace, and go onto the canal towpath through the nearest gate in the railing. Pass the former toll house, now the British Waterways London Region Office, staying on the cobbled towpath under the bridge. Walk alongside Little Venice, passing opposite the small island in the middle, whose willow trees are a waterfowl refuge. Just before the towpath leads you down the Paddington Arm of the canal, turn right up a set of steps and turn left into Warwick Crescent.

③ At the end, ahead to the left is the HQ of the fashion chain Monsoon, in the refurbished listed 1960s goods yard maintenance building, sandwiched between the road and the flyover. Turn left, cross Warwick Avenue and go straight on down Howley Place. Turn right and continue along St Mary's Terrace into St Mary's Square. Pass the left of the church hall with classical-style trompe l'oeil paintings – they really are flat.

④ Walk round to the right of St Mary's, coming back to Church Yard Walk. Cross this and go through the gates into the north part of the churchyard, which has been parkland since 1895. Take the path on the right hand side. The grave on the right enclosed by railings, with a glass roof, is that of Sarah Siddons, the country's

---

PLACES OF INTEREST NEARBY

The **Alexander Fleming Laboratory Museum** in St Mary's Hospital, Praed Street (near Paddington Station) is in the very place where Fleming discovered penicillin. Open from Monday to Thursday (not bank holidays) between 10 am and 1 pm, other times by appointment. Telephone: 020 7886 6528.

A colourful canalside garden in Little Venice

leading tragic actress in the late 18th and early 19th centuries. Pass this and leave the park at the north-east end through the gate, and follow the path past the school to Crompton Street. Turn left at Edgware Road and cross Maida Avenue and the canal. On the bridge is a restaurant whose terrace gives an excellent view of the boats waiting to enter the tunnel.

⑤ Turn left onto Blomfield Road. Don't go through the gate onto the path by the moorings, but walk on the footpath just to the left of the line of trees. Admire the elaborately painted house-boats here. Cross Warwick

Avenue with care, and continue past Little Venice, passing the entrances to the floating gallery and restaurant. Continue along and turn right into Warwick Place to return to the pub.

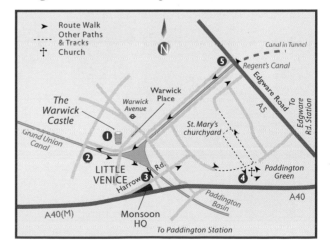

Finchley
The Catcher in the Rye

MAP: OS EXPLORER 173 (GR 250905)   **WALK 26**   **DISTANCE:** 4 MILES

DIRECTIONS TO START: THE PUB IS AT 317 REGENT'S PARK ROAD (A598) NEAR THE JUNCTION WITH HENDON LANE, JUST SOUTH OF THE STATION. **STATION:** FINCHLEY CENTRAL (NORTHERN). **PARKING:** THERE IS NO PUB CAR PARK; THERE IS STREET PARKING JUST SOUTH OF COLLEGE TERRACE. AT WEEKENDS TRY FINCHLEY CENTRAL CAR PARK, OR IN FRONT OF AVENUE HOUSE.

The walk takes you first through a pleasant older part of Finchley, past terraced houses and the 15th century local church. You then continue onto a marvellous green corridor by Dollis Brook, lined with willow and other trees. The route continues alongside Mutton Brook, right next to the A1/North Circular roads, but the brook is lined by ivy-covered hawthorn, beech, willow, sycamore and oak, providing a varied wild habitat. Finally, the grounds of Avenue House, now a public park, formerly belonged to the house owned by the Stephens of Stephens Inks, and contain some interesting trees.

The Catcher in the Rye

This is a pub with a terrific name, and a good range of beers: Adnams Broadside, Greene King, a seasonal Brakspear ale, such as Leaf Fall, and a monthly guest ale. There are several bars, some with comfortable soft seats – in the window is a good place. Food is served from 12 noon to 9 pm Monday to Friday, to 8 pm on Saturday and to 6 pm on Sunday. Sandwiches and small dishes are available, as well as main courses which come in huge portions. The home-made chips served with some dishes are good, but the star attraction is sausage and mash. The desserts are tasty, unhealthy and will round off the meal (and you). Telephone: 020 8343 4369.

The Walk

① Leave the pub, turn right then right again into College Terrace. Cross Hendon Lane, then turn right into St Mary's churchyard. Walk through it, leaving via the pathway at the far left end. Turn left at the road, Church Crescent, and follow this round to the right. Continue over Dollis Avenue down the footpath opposite. Cross over the next road and continue down the path opposite (just to the left). This is tree-lined and fenced, between sports fields. Over to the right is the Northern Line viaduct on the Mill Hill branch, the highest point above ground level on the underground.

② Turn left just before Dollis Brook, onto the Dollis Valley Greenwalk (DVG). The path is good by the stream, which itself is kept wild, despite the closeness of housing. Cross over another path, leading to a footbridge, and enter Windsor Open Space, an expanse of grass and trees. Pass another footbridge on the right and a play area on the left. The Open Space ends; continue on the narrow path by the stream.

③ Cross Waverley Grove, staying beside the stream. Fork left to go through the subway under the next road to Hendon Lane Weir, and continue past the island in the brook. Go under the next road bridge, the A1, which has the Middlesex arms on the parapet. Do not cross the next footbridge over a stream, Mutton Brook, coming from the left.

④ Turn left here, following the DVG signs along the Mutton Brook. Go through another subway, under the North Circular Road. Come out into a wide grassy area bounded by the combined might of the A1 and North Circular on one side, and the brook on the other. Come to Finchley Road. Up to the left, across the main road,

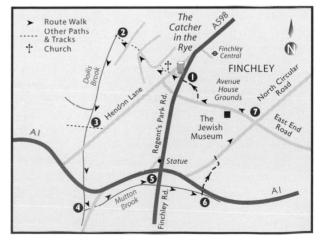

Dollis Valley Greenwalk

at the north end of Charter Green, is a bronze statue from 1920, *La Délivrance*, known locally as The Naked Lady.

⑤ Cross Finchley Road and continue opposite down the tarmac path, following DVG and Capital Ring arrows, back towards the brook. Cross the footbridge and continue with the brook on your left through the trees. At the road, continue on the tarmac path back down towards the stream. Beyond it is a broad meadow and the main road. Pass a small weir; the meadow over the brook ends and the path on the other side is clearly visible.

⑥ At a footbridge turn left, ignoring the DVG and Capital Ring arrows, and turn right up to the road. Turn left and then right, crossing the A1 at the island refuge and continuing straight up Beaufort Drive. At the end, turn right into Connaught Drive, then immediately left towards the footbridge. Cross it, taking in the views over the North Circular, then continue uphill by the fenced-off A406. At the end of Amberden Road, the North Circular is

in a cutting. Continue along the bush-lined path.

⑦ Turn left at East End Road. Pass the end of Manor View on the right, then the Sternberg Centre on the left. Cross over. At the end of the sports ground on the right, go through the gate into Avenue House grounds. Turn left, walk to the house, then turn right. Take a right fork uphill onto a fir-topped mound, then descend and turn left onto a main path. Leave the grounds through the gate, go up the track to Regent's Park Road, then turn right to return to the pub.

PLACES OF INTEREST NEARBY

The **Jewish Museum**, at the Sternberg Centre on the route of the walk, has reconstructions of an East End tailor's and a cabinet maker's workshop, a Holocaust education gallery, and special exhibitions. Admission charge. Open to 5 pm on Monday to Thursday and 4.30 pm on Sundays. Closed Friday and Saturday, and also closed on Jewish festivals and Sundays in August. Telephone: 020 8349 1143.

West Finchley
The Elephant

DIRECTIONS TO START: THE PUB IS AT 283 BALLARDS LANE, CLOSE TO THE JUNCTION WITH THE A1000 HIGH ROAD, AT THE CORNER OF HUTTON GROVE. **STATION:** WEST FINCHLEY (NORTHERN LINE). **PARKING:** THE PUB HAS NO CAR PARK; TRY ON-STREET IN THE VICINITY. THERE ARE PAY CAR PARKS NEAR TALLY HO CORNER, WHERE THE A1000 MEETS BALLARDS LANE.

The Mill Hill area has open land that feels as if it is far away in the countryside, only a few minutes from the Northern Line. Part of the route is a very pretty path through rural-feeling fields with plenty of wild plants. Brambles line the edges of fields – it's a great place for blackberrying in late summer. Woodridge Nature Reserve is a haven for insects and birds along the line of Folly Brook. Dollis Brook provides another green corridor through this area.

The Elephant

This is a large welcoming Fuller's pub with a patio and tables at the front for fine weather. Inside, a quiet carpeted saloon bar on the right adjoins a separate dining area. There is another bar on the left with sport on a large screen TV. Naturally, Fuller's London Pride and ESB are on draught, together with one of Fuller's seasonal brews, such as Organic Honey Dew in the spring, or delicious Jack Frost in winter.

You can eat in either the bar or the restaurant area – Ben's Thai Restaurant. Food is available at lunchtime and evenings from 12 noon to 2.30 pm and 6 pm to 10 pm, with the house speciality obviously being Thai food. English food is available (including jumbo sausage, disappointingly not called a house speciality) but the aromatic crispy Thai food prepared from fresh ingredients is terrific, and definitely the best choice. Now, the hottest meal we have ever had was in a Thai restaurant, but don't be afraid – the menu indicates which dishes are hot or spicy. Have a Thai dessert as well. Telephone: 020 8492 0201.

The Walk

① Turn right leaving the pub onto Ballards Lane, then turn right again into Alexandra Grove. Cross Nether Street and continue on into Argyle Road, under the railway bridge and then over the stream. Immediately over the bridge, the road once more changes its name to Lullington Garth; turn left through the railing onto Riverside Walk – the Dollis Valley Greenwalk (DVG), also signposted 'Leisure Walk 3'.

② Follow this path on the right of Dollis Brook through parkland-style open space, which preserves some wilderness next to the brook. At the next road, Fursby Avenue, leave the fenced space, cross the road, turn right then immediately left back into green space following the DVG and Leisure Walk 3 arrows. Follow the tarmac path between allotments, then a wilderness area beside the brook.

③ At a footbridge on your left, turn right onto Lovers Walk. Follow this lane between two parts of Finchley Golf Course, with a stream on your right. You are sheltered from golf balls by hawthorn, chestnut and oak trees and shrubbery – far more variety than the golf course. At a fork, keep straight on, pass the golf club car park and a line of fir trees, and exit The Paddocks to turn right onto Frith Lane. At a fork in the road, turn left onto Partingdale Lane, go through the gate in the lane, then just after turn right at a metal gate down the 'Public Bridleway to Burtonhole' (not into Frith Manor Orchard just to the right of it).

④ Follow the bridleway, a wide and occasionally muddy track, through countryside and woods to a T-junction; turn right at the sign 'public footpath Totteridge ¾'. There is also an arrow on the

PLACES OF INTEREST NEARBY

The local nature reserve at **Coppetts Wood**, managed by the Borough of Barnet, includes woodland and scrubland. There is a nature trail – leaflets are available from Barnet libraries or by calling 020 8359 4478. There is a small car park off Colney Hatch Lane, off Woodhouse Road (A1003).

On the route

on the left of the brook. You may see squirrels chasing each other through the brambles and nettles. Continue out of the reserve through a gateway, pass a sports ground and clubhouse on the left and at the end turn right onto Southover.

⑥ Cross this road at a central traffic island and go through the gate following arrows for Barnet Leisure Walks 2 and 3 to reach the Riverside Walk, Dollis Valley Greenwalk. The grass is mown short, but the side of the brook is wild. Follow the tarmac path, past plenty of trees, and go through the gate onto Lullington Garth. Now retrace your steps across Dollis Brook, going up Argyle Road and turning left at the end of Alexandra Grove to return to the pub.

adjacent kissing gate 'Barnet Countryside Leisure Walks 3'. Follow the path along the left hand side of the field, past blackberry bushes and fine views to the right.

⑤ At the bridge over Folly Brook, turn right at the stile, following the arrows to Woodridge Nature Reserve. Cross another stile into the nature reserve, and follow the path through the open meadow, which is surrounded by trees and undergrowth. Continue through a wooded area of willow and oak trees

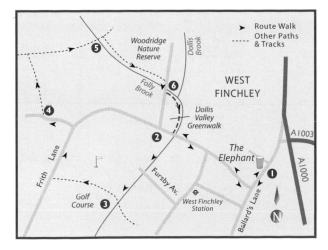

New Barnet
The Builders Arms

| MAP: OS EXPLORER 173 (265962) | **WALK 28** | DISTANCE: 2¼ MILES |

DIRECTIONS TO START: THE PUB IS ON ALBERT ROAD. FROM THE A110 TURN NORTH
ONTO ALBERT ROAD JUST EAST OF THE RAILWAY BRIDGE IN NEW BARNET.
STATION: NEW BARNET. **PARKING:** THERE IS NO PUB CAR PARK, BUT TRY
SURROUNDING STREETS. ALTERNATIVELY, USE THE CAR PARK AT THE EASTERN END OF
BAKERS HILL AND START AT POINT 5.

Much of this walk goes through the meadows and the ancient oak and beech woods of Monken Hadley Common. Once part of the great royal hunting forest of Enfield Chase, this has remained a peaceful open space of timeless natural beauty.

The area around Beech Hill Lake is an excellent place to spot several varieties of bats feeding on balmy summer evenings. You'll also encounter the path of Pymmes Brook, which forms a green corridor into the built-up areas of London.

The Builders Arms

This characterful little pub occupies a building that was once two adjoining railway cottages, built in the 19th century when the railway came to New Barnet. The cosy lounge bar, reached through the door on the left, is carpeted and has wood-panelled walls and comfortable upholstered furniture. No music is played and locals from all walks of life spend hours here, some doing crosswords, hence the collection of battered old dictionaries and thesauruses on the bookcase to the left of the bar. The public bar, reached through the door on the left, is a less cerebral milieu, being much rowdier with a juke box and games.

The pub is a Greene King house with Ruddles County and Greene King IPA on handpump. The menu includes sausages with mash and onion in gravy, chilli con carne, scampi and chips, filled jacket potatoes, sandwiches, burgers, omelettes, salads and pasta dishes. The Builders Arms is open during standard pub hours and food is served from 12 noon to 3 pm from Monday to Friday. Telephone: 020 8216 5678. There is no food at weekends so if you want to eat on Saturday or Sunday try the Railway Bell in East Barnet Road. Telephone: 020 8440 1369.

The Walk

① Leaving the pub, turn left and follow the road as it curves right. Turn left at the T-junction onto Victoria Road. Take the first left onto a tarmac track signposted to Lawton Road. Continue along this track into a recreation ground. Cross a bridge

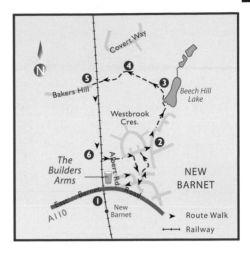

over a stream and turn right onto a narrow tarmac path near the left side of the stream, following it around as it turns left. At a fountain in the middle of a circle of crazy paving, veer slightly right, passing a bowling green and then tennis courts on the right and a playing field on the left. At the fork at the end of the tennis courts veer right and continue ahead, passing a playground on the left, to exit onto Lawton Road. Turn right.

② At the T-junction cross over and turn left to walk along the grass, following a Pymmes Brook Trail sign. Walk along the grass on the right side of Baring Road. When the road curves right, go straight ahead on the shrub-fringed footpath, still following the Pymmes Brook Trail sign on a wooden post. Go through a wooden kissing gate to a T-junction with a three-ways sign. Turn right, cross Pymmes Brook by a brick and stone bridge, turn left and take a concrete footbridge over a ditch. Veer left and then right to go up seven steps to Beech Hill Lake. Turn left and go ahead across a wooden footbridge.

Beech Hill Lake

③ Fork slightly left to walk away from the lake. At the T-junction fork right and continue past a meadow on the right and shrubbery on the left. Stay close to the shrubs and trees on the left, but ignore paths into them.

④ Just short of a lone oak tree in the meadow on your right, and shortly before the periphery of the meadow veers right, turn sharp left onto a narrow path into the wood, soon veering right with the path. Keep going along this curving woodland path and soon you pass wooden fencing on the left. Turn left to go through the kissing gate in this fencing. Ignore a crosspath and keep going ahead. At the T-junction turn right. Eventually veer left down eleven wide wooden steps. At the bottom continue ahead over a railway bridge.

⑤ Go through the gap to the left of a wide metal gate and turn immediately left, onto a path with a railway line on the left. Continue past a golf course on the right and then houses on the right.

⑥ At a tarmac crosspath turn left up steps and go through a tunnel under the railway. Take a walkway over the grounds of an office block and then down steps. Turn right through a gate into the recreation ground you walked through earlier. Turn immediately left along the periphery path, passing a gas tank on the left. Turn right on a tarmac track, following a footpath sign leading to Victoria Road. Cross the bridge over Pymmes Brook to leave the park. At the T-junction with Victoria Road, turn right towards the railway bridge. Just before the bridge, turn right onto Albert Road and back to the pub.

PLACES OF INTEREST NEARBY
The **Barnet Museum**, at 31 Wood Street (A411) tells the history of the area from 1471, when the Battle of Barnet played a decisive role in ending the Wars of the Roses. There are fascinating displays of social history and the decorative arts. Opening times are from 2.30 pm to 4.30 pm on Tuesday to Thursday; 10 am to 12 noon and 2.30 pm to 4.30 pm on Saturday. Telephone: 020 8440 8066.

Chelsea
The Coopers Arms

MAP: OS EXPLORER 161 (GR 275779) | **WALK 29** | **DISTANCE:** 2½ MILES

DIRECTIONS TO START: COMING DOWN KINGS ROAD FROM SLOANE SQUARE, TURN LEFT INTO FLOOD STREET. THE PUB IS AT THE CORNER WITH REDESDALE STREET. **STATIONS:** SLOANE SQUARE (CIRCLE AND DISTRICT LINES); BATTERSEA PARK (SUBURBAN RAIL). **PARKING:** THE PUB HAS NO CAR PARK. THERE IS PARKING IN BATTERSEA PARK.

The star attraction of this walk round some delights of Chelsea is Chelsea Physic Garden, named for physicians, not physics. The garden is three and a half acres of medicinal plants, founded in 1673 by the Society of Apothecaries. The walled garden in this built-up part of Chelsea has a warm microclimate, and many delicate plants flourish. It is open to the public on Wednesday (12 noon to 5 pm) and Sunday (2 pm to 6 pm) afternoons from April to October (admission fee, free to Friends, who may also visit during Monday to Friday working

hours). Check on 020 7352 5646.

You cross the river on the elegant Albert Bridge and walk through Battersea Park, one of the first public parks in Britain, home of the 1951 Festival Gardens, now being restored. Returning to the north bank, you walk through the grounds of Wren's spectacular Royal Hospital, Chelsea. The grounds are open from 10 am (2 pm on Sundays) until 8.30 pm in summer, closing earlier (4.30 pm) with the shorter days in November to March. Check on 020 7881 5246 (office hours).

The Coopers Arms

The pub is a friendly refuge from Kings Road. The cavernous interior of bare floorboards and battered wooden tables has a laid-back feeling – newspapers are provided, there's no background music and there's a table for diners to help themselves to bread. Older regulars congregate at the bar, and the younger set chat at tables. Beers are Young's ales – Best Bitter, Waggle Dance, Special and Triple A – plus Hoegaarden and there are lots of wines, sparkling wines and champagne.

The excellent food is chosen from a changing menu, and may include delights such as grilled scallops, Parmesan-crusted herring, smoked salmon and scrambled eggs, and also upmarket versions of pub dishes such as sausage and mash with spring onions and onion gravy or Coopers cottage pie topped with cheese. Finish with some really tempting desserts, like Florida orange sponge. Food is served every day from 12 noon to 3 pm and from 6.30 pm to 9.30 pm, except Sunday evenings. The pub opening times are Monday to Saturday from 11 am to 11 pm, Sunday from 12 noon to 10.30 pm. Telephone: 020 7376 3120.

The Walk

① From the pub turn left onto Flood Street. Turn left into Robinson Street, and at Christchurch, turn right into Christchurch Street. Walk on the left hand side to get a view of the primary school, part of which is in a 19th century National Schools building. Continue down to Royal Hospital Road, cross, turn left, and turn right into Swan Walk.

② In Swan Walk, turn right into Chelsea Physic Garden. Walk round the garden (guided tours are available), taking in the south gate facing the river. Leave via the exit on Royal Hospital Road, turn left, walk via Cheyne Walk or Chelsea Embankment to Albert Bridge and cross it. Admire the ironwork and views as you do.

③ At the far end, turn left into Battersea Park, following the riverside walk. Pass the 1985 Peace Pagoda built by Japanese Buddhists, with four statues of stages in the life of Buddha. At the end of the park is a view of Battersea power station. Turn left onto Queenstown Road. Cross Chelsea Bridge. Cross the busy Chelsea Embankment at the lights towards the Carabiniers Boer War memorial and turn left.

④ At the Bullring gate, turn left into the Royal Hospital grounds. Walk towards the monument, and take the first right towards the avenue of plane trees. Turn left down the avenue, approaching the rear side of the hospital, then pass by the museum and shop, and entrances to the Great Hall, Chapel and courts to leave the grounds, noting the small burial ground on the right.

PLACES OF INTEREST NEARBY

The **National Army Museum** on Royal Hospital Road, between the Royal Hospital and the Physic Garden, covers 500 years of the history of the British Army and its campaigns. Displays include uniforms, scale models, specially commissioned short films, and exhibits such as cannons and the skeleton of Napoleon's horse Marengo. The museum is open from 10 am to 5.30 pm every day except some bank holidays; check on 020 7730 0717. Admission free.

Chelsea Physic Garden

⑤ Go down Franklin's Row opposite, and at the end of the Court, turn left onto St Leonard's Terrace. Number 18 was the home of Bram Stoker, author of *Dracula*, and yes, this is just minutes from a burial ground. Continue along through the top end of Tedworth Square into Redesdale Street to return to the pub.

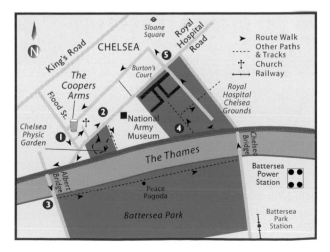

Southgate
The Woodman

MAP: OS EXPLORER 173 (GR 306938)   **WALK 30**   **DISTANCE:** 3½ MILES

DIRECTIONS TO START: FROM THE NORTH CIRCULAR ROAD TAKE THE A105 NORTH FOR NEARLY ONE MILE, THEN TURN LEFT ONTO THE A111, BOURNE HILL. **STATIONS:** SOUTHGATE (PICCADILLY; BUS W9 FROM THE STATION), WINCHMORE HILL (SUBURBAN RAIL). **PARKING:** IN THE PUB CAR PARK (PLEASE ASK FIRST); THERE IS A SMALL FREE CAR PARK NEAR THE PARK GATES.

Very close to each other in the Southgate part of Enfield are two large public parks, purchased for the public at the beginning of the 20th century. Both were originally part of Enfield Chase, which was deforested in 1777, and the land was then split up. Grovelands Park was the grounds of the large 18th century house that is now a private hospital in one corner. The public park now has neatly mown areas and wilder parts accommodating lots of wildlife, together with a large lake.

Oakwood Park was two properties before it became a public park. It is now wonderful open parkland with lines of mature trees, including an oak avenue, together with hedgerow plants like hawthorn, which show the old field boundaries. Both parks are maintained by the Borough of Enfield; Grovelands Park has a café and toilets near the lake.

The Woodman

The Woodman has an attractive position up Bourne Hill, with a rural feeling. At the front, in the original older part, there is a small cosy smoky bar, with a larger bar and patio further through, together with a pleasant conservatory dining area, which bans smoking and mobile phones. Worthington and Bass ales are available, and there is a wine list.

A printed menu offers a choice of food ranging from sandwiches and ploughman's lunches to full three-course meals and coffee. The main courses include good hefty steaks and fish, together with traditional pub favourites, jacket potatoes, vegetarian options and full Sunday lunches. Children are welcome in the conservatory and patio, which is next to climbing frames, and a garden area. The pub is open all day. Food is served from 11 am to 2.30 pm and from 6 pm to 8.30 pm on Monday to Saturday and from 12 noon to about 4 pm on Sunday. Telephone: 020 8882 0294.

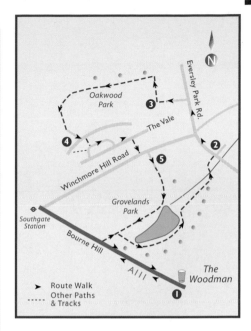

The Walk

① Turn right out of the pub down Bourne Hill. Turn right through the main gates into Grovelands Park. Turn right down a small avenue past the pitch and putt course towards the lake, then walk round the lake, keeping it on your left, to go through the wilder part. Pass a children's play area and café (open April to September). Further round the lake there is a view of Grovelands House. Then take a gravel path leading off to the right away from the lake downhill through the woods to a watercourse. Follow the stream past three footbridges, and cross over a tarmac path (leading to gates on the right). Continue on a possibly muddy path to the right of the trees – the stream has now gone underground. Turn left onto a tarmac path, then turn right to leave the park through the gates opposite Stone Hall Road.

② Turn left up Church Hill. Go straight over a crossroads into Eversley Park Road, an oak-lined road. Turn left into Willow Walk, continuing into Oakwood Park.

③ Turn right to go up the tarmac path, then turn left onto a grassy path running south of a pitch and putt course. Turn half left onto a small tarmac path and go downhill through the wooded area. You see a children's play area, then turn left onto a tarmac path leading down to the exit.

Grovelands Park

④ Come out of the park, cross Oakwood Park Road and continue down the alleyway opposite, then turn left and walk between the double hedges of Fountains Crescent. Turn left into The Vale, cross it, then shortly after turn right into the alley between 92 and 94. Turn left at Winchmore Hill Road and then right into Park Gate.

⑤ Go back into Grovelands Park, and head out to the half right across the grass, making for the lake. Keep it on your left, then head for the park gate. Leave through this and turn left to return to the pub.

PLACES OF INTEREST NEARBY

Just a few minutes' walk north of Oakwood Park, **Boxer's Lake** on Lonsdale Drive, reached via Prince George Avenue and Kenwood Avenue, has been the subject of attention because of the size of carp it contained. This even sparked a children's poetry competition on the BBC. It has now apparently been over-fished, so leave your rod at home.